FOR YOUNG VOICES

SOMETHING NEW TO SING ABOUT

STUDENT TEXT

Glencoe

G. SCHIRMER, Inc.

The Complete Series

SOMETHING NEW TO SING ABOUT FOR YOUNG VOICES:
(A revision of SOMETHING TO SING ABOUT FOR YOUNG VOICES)

Choral Literature
2 part, SSA, Male ensembles
ISBN 0-02-642071-6
Rehearsal Accompaniment Cassette Tape for above
ISBN 0-02-642090-2

Choral Literature
SAB, SATB (SACB)
ISBN 0-02-642070-8
Rehearsal Accompaniment Cassette Tape for above
ISBN 0-02-642080-5

Student Text
ISBN 0-02-642076-7

Teacher's Binder
ISBN 0-02-642073-2

Teacher's Manual
ISBN 0-02-642075-9

SOMETHING TO SING ABOUT:

For Young Voices
ISBN 0-02-642050-3
Level I
ISBN 0-02-642010-4
Level II
ISBN 0-02-642020-1
Level III
ISBN 0-02-642030-9
Student Workbook
ISBN 0-02-642040-6
Teacher's Manual
ISBN 0-02-642060-0
(for Levels I, II, III and Young Voices)

Glencoe

Contributing Authors

Dr. William V. May
Senior Editor

Coordinator of Music Education
North Texas State University
Denton, Texas

Mary Kay Beall

Music Education Specialist
Lyricist; Associate Editor, Somerset Press
(Educational Division of Hope Publishing Co.)

Dr. Gene Cho

Coordinator of Music Theory
North Texas State University
Denton, Texas

Dennis Hendrickson

Director of Choral Activities
Atlantic Public Schools
Atlantic, Iowa

Melinda Hendrickson

Music Educator
Atlantic Public Schools
Atlantic, Iowa

Margaret Hudnall

North Texas State University
Denton, Texas

Jeanne Opitz

Music Educator
Waukesha Public Schools
Waukesha, Wisconsin

Barbara Thomas

Lamar University
Beaumont, Texas

Richard Walters

Supervising Editor, G. Schirmer Division
Hal Leonard Publishing Corp.

Special Contributors:

Dr. Steve Brown
Dana Lobaugh
Diane Penny
Michael Turner

PREFACE

Everyone—everyone has "Something to Sing About." Singing with the human voice is perhaps our oldest way of making music. It is an activity in which millions of people participate each day. People sing when they are happy, when they are sad, when they have a difficult idea to express, when they want to remember their history, and when they just want to have fun. People sing now and they have always sung. Anthropologists, those scientists which study the nature of mankind, have provided us with a remarkable finding. It seems that every culture, every social group, every society about which we know in the history of mankind had singing as a part of their culture. When one thinks just how many differences among people exist—different language, different customs, different religions, different diets, different ways of living—it is truly amazing that all of those people in history would do any single thing. Yet they all sang and continue to sing. We don't really know why this is true; however, we can guess that it is because singing is such a natural, wonderful activity.

Can anyone enjoy singing in some way? Yes! Few other human activities are simple enough for a small child to enjoy yet challenging enough for a scholar to spend a lifetime studying. Whether as a participant or listener, in groups or as a soloist, at school or at home, Everyone has "Something to Sing About!" Won't you join in the song?

W. May, Senior Editor

CONTENTS

Something New To Sing About

THE VOICE

The human voice is a rare gift of nature. Its primary function, as in other animals, is to keep foreign particles out of the lungs, but it also functions as a means of communication and can be a vehicle for artistic forms. Singing is one of the highest forms of art, requiring mental, physical, and emotional effort and control. Using one's voice correctly to produce beautiful musical sounds demands time, mental concentration, physical training, and regular practice.

The singing process is triggered by a command from the brain to begin a complex series of physical actions. Controlled respiration occurs, the vocal cords are brought together and begin to vibrate as air passes from the lungs through the glottis. The pharynx, mouth, and tongue are shaped to form the given sound, as teeth and lips add the final articulation. Tones become intelligible sounds when the sound is shaped to produce specific vowel and consonant sounds.

When singing, the vocalist must be concerned with all the musical aspects of sound. Correct pitch, duration, and loudness for each note must be produced. Precise attacks and releases must be performed. While producing tone quality appropriate for the music, the singer also must attend to the clarity of each word. Training the voice to accomplish all of this at once is a challenge which requires a positive attitude, disciplined energy, and diligent study.

BREATHING AND POSTURE

Relaxed, normal breathing is a simple process requiring no conscious thought, but control of respiration for specific tasks demands complicated adjustments within the body. Singing requires utmost efficiency both for inspiration and for controlled expiration. Since efficient breathing begins with good body alignment, posture must be the first consideration. Although some postures may seem relaxed, if the body is out of alignment, undue strain is placed on the skeleton and then muscles cannot function easily and effectively.

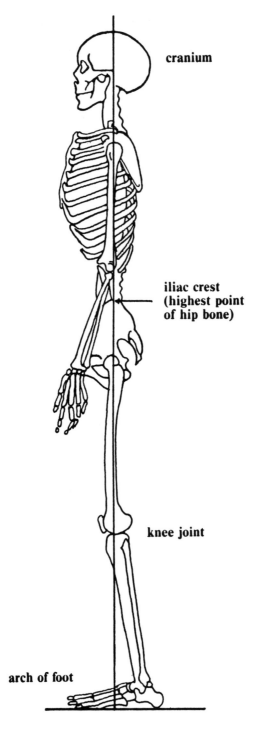

cranium

iliac crest
(highest point
of hip bone)

knee joint

arch of foot

GOOD BODY ALIGNMENT

A good vocalist constantly will be careful to maintain proper posture for singing. The following hints may serve as checkpoints:

1. Standing with feet slightly apart for good balance
2. Relaxed, unlocked knees
3. Chest held comfortably high
4. Shoulders back, but relaxed
5. Arms and hands relaxed and hanging loosely at sides
6. Head straight on neck with crown of head the highest point

When holding music, the singer should try to keep tension from creeping up the arms into the shoulders and neck. Music should be held high enough to allow the proper position for the head. If singers must sit while performing, they should sit forward in the chair with both feet on the floor. Careful attention should then be given to upper body and head postures. (No. 3-5 above)

POOR SINGING POSTURES

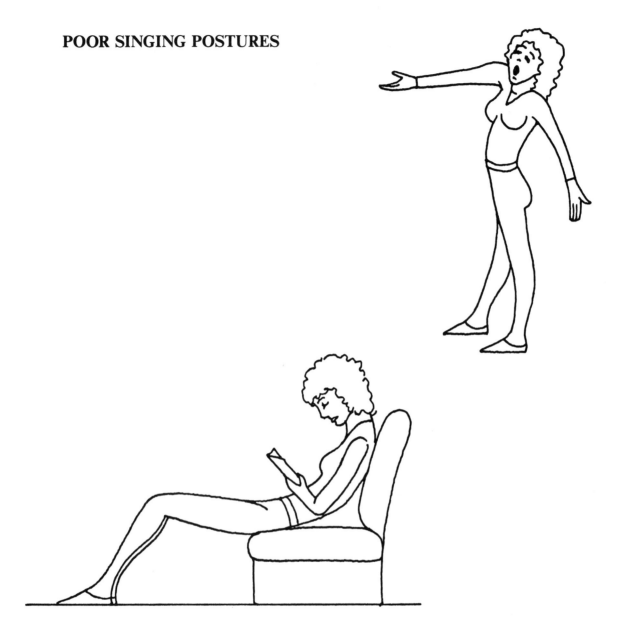

Once good posture is established, the singer should be able to breathe quietly while filling the lungs deeply. To do this the diaphragm must contract completely, and the ribs should expand. To learn this manner of breathing, the singer may concentrate on expanding the ribs at the sides and in back while breathing slowly through the nose. For versatility in attack and dynamic level, it is well if the singer can learn to breathe simultaneously through the mouth and nose for a quick, deep breath. The throat should always be kept open to prevent tension and noisy inhalation. For controlled expiration the singer may concentrate on these actions and sensations:

1. Keeping the chest high, not allowing it to sink as air leaves the lungs
2. Feeling the abdominal muscles working against the waist band to control the amount of air exhaled
3. Keeping the ribs expanded as long as possible while gradually relaxing the diaphragm

Exercise for practicing good breathing habits:

1. Inhale slowly while mentally counting to five.
2. On a comfortable pitch count to ten slowly.
3. Each day try for a higher count until reaching thirty or above.

VOCAL PRODUCTION

When a person uses the breath to sing, the air travels from the lungs through the trachea to the larynx (pronounced larinks, not larnicks)—the area where the sound is produced. The larynx includes cartilages and bones to which the muscles that control sound production are attached. Across the top of the trachea, the vocal folds (sometimes called "cords", but they do not resemble most people's image of a cord) grow, connected in front to the thyroid cartilage and in back to the arytenoid cartilages. At the moment that a sound is to be made, the muscles of the arytenoid cartilages bring the vocal folds together, in much the same way as one might stretch the top of a balloon to make it squeal as air rushes out. As air passes through the vocal folds, the tissue is set in motion (vibration) and sound is produced. Once the sound is produced, the air around the vocal folds is set into motion. These "waves of sound" are adjusted by the resonating cavities, primarily the pharynx, and pass through the air to the listener's ear. This adjustment process gives to voice its particular timbre.

The pitch of the newly created sound depends on the thickness and the length of the vocal folds plus the amount of tension created by stretching the folds between the thyroid and arytenoid cartilages. The greater the thickness and length, the lower the pitch and vice versa. The greater the tension, the higher the pitch and vice versa. The loudness of the sound is determined by the amount and speed of the air passing through the folds. One must remember that the muscles of the larynx are very small. Minor changes in their position make major differences in pitch. If a student's vocal folds are slightly smaller than another student's, the first student will have a higher voice.

VOICE QUALITY: RESONANCE AND PHARYNGEAL POSTURE

Quality of sound is directly related to the shape of the resonator. For example, two strings of equal size, length, thickness, and tension sound different if plucked when one is stretched across two nails in a board and the other is stretched across the sound hole of a guitar. It is the difference in resonating chamber that makes the difference in timbre. In singing, resonation is determined by the posture of the pharynx. The pharynx is a space which can be divided into three areas:

the **nasal pharynx**—the area from the nostrils to the soft palate

the **oral pharynx**—the space from the soft palate to the epiglottis including the mouth, tongue, and throat

the **laryngeal pharynx**—the area from the epiglottis (opening of the larynx) to the cricoid cartilage

11

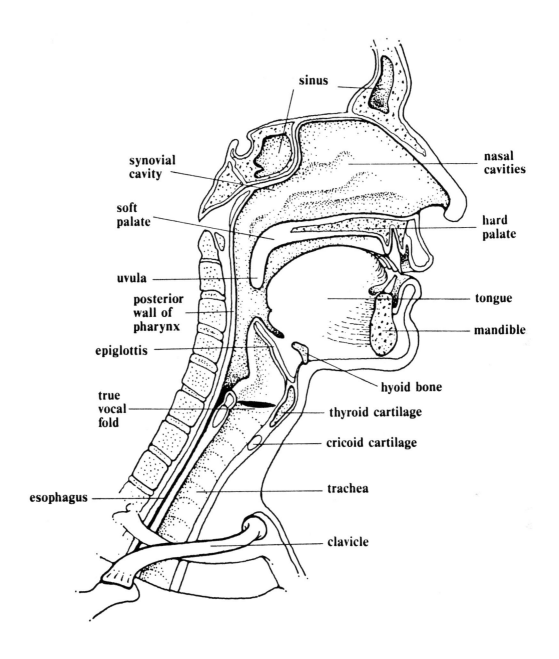

sinus

nasal
cavities

synovial
cavity

soft
palate

hard
palate

uvula

tongue

posterior
wall of
pharynx

mandible

epiglottis

hyoid bone

true
vocal
fold

thyroid cartilage

cricoid cartilage

trachea

esophagus

clavicle

The largest and most easily adjusted part of the pharynx is the oral pharynx. By making changes in the position of the soft palate, the tongue, the jaw, and lips the singer forms different sounds and qualities of tone (timbres). Undesirable tone qualities described as "harsh, nasal, throaty, or breathy" can usually be eliminated by attending to oral pharyngeal posture. Although changes must take place for each vowel and consonant, these general rules will aid "inside" singing posture:

1. Keep tip of tongue lightly against the bottom teeth. The root of the tongue is directly attached to the epiglottis. When the tongue is held too far back, it can cause great tension in the larynx and a harsh, overly dark, throaty sound.

2. Keep jaw relaxed. Never let it jut forward. The position of the jaw greatly affects posture in the larynx as well as the pharynx and, if misplaced, keeps the laryngeal muscles from working properly.

3. Try to gently stretch the oral pharynx: feel a lift right behind the cheeks, in the roof of the mouth, and at the back of the throat (not in the lower part of the throat).

4. Keep a lifted soft palate when possible. This keeps the sound from taking on the resonance characteristics of the nasal pharynx, a "nasal" quality. The palate is lifted for all vowel sounds although closure is not always complete. The palate is slightly lower for sounds such as [m] and [n].

5. Keep the lips relaxed, never tense. Be especially careful when rounding or stretching the lips as required for some vowels and consonants.

DICTION AND FACIAL POSTURE

VOWEL PRODUCTION

While maintaining good tone quality, the singer must also produce intelligible sounds which are classified as vowels and consonants. To form beautiful but understandable vowels is perhaps the most important aspect of singing. Unfortunately this also is one of the most difficult elements of singing, particularly when English is the student's mother tongue. English includes many different vowel sounds and vowel combinations which are used in proper pronunciation. If one adds to this list the many improper vowels for singing which are products of regional dialects, the problem for the teacher is greatly compounded. The addition of foreign languages to the singer's repertory creates further difficulties.

In order to simplify the learning process, the inexperienced singer is best served by initially focussing on three vowel sounds: ah [ɑ] as in father; ee [i] as in bee; and oo [u] as in too. These represent the three fundamental vowel sounds common to most languages. When proper production of these basic vowel sounds is achieved, the other vowel sounds become much easier to produce.

These three vowels (a,i,u) should be practiced until they are formed correctly. The following illustration shows facial postures which may help singers in gaining the desired sound. Facial structures are different, as is the size of teeth, lips, etc. Some differences will be noted on each singer, but in general these facial postures should enhance both pharyngeal and laryngeal postures. Some practice with a mirror may be necessary, so that the singer may quickly and easily produce each sound with the recommended facial appearance.

Mirror, mirror on the wall,
Who are the best singers of all?

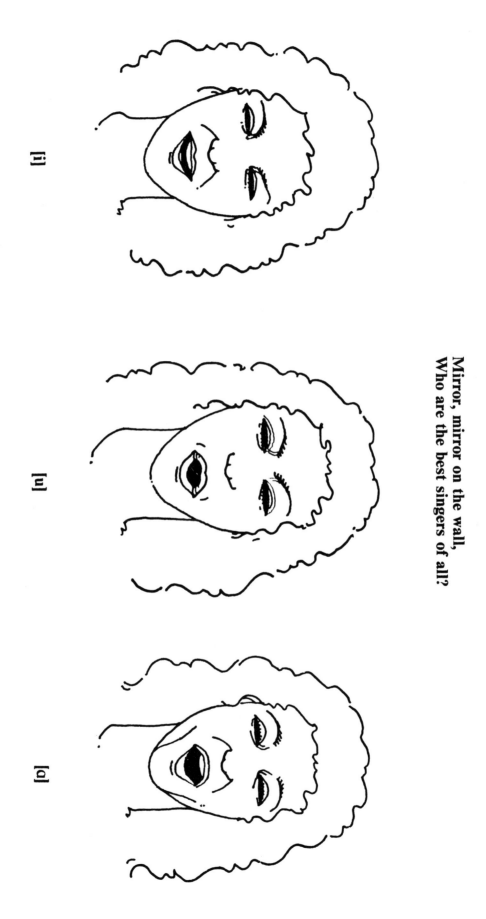

[i]

[u]

[ɑ]

Attention should be paid to the following facial postures when producing the fundamental vowels, as shown in the prior illustration.

  I. [ɑ]   Drop jaw. Keep it relaxed, free and never jutted forward.
     (ah)   Place tip of tongue against bottom teeth.
              Lift cheeks. Allow upper teeth to show slightly.
 II. [i]   Allow both sets of teeth to show, but keep corners of the mouth
     (ee)   relaxed.
              This is the most "East & West" position, but think a little "North &
              South" for jaw and lips.
III. [u]   Relax jaw.
     (oo)   Sink in cheeks.
              Round lips (no tension!).
              Have a feeling of lots of space in the mouth.

The soft palate should be completely lifted and the throat open on all vowels (like the beginning of a yawn).

When first practicing these facial positions, the student is cautioned against "overdoing" any of the directions. In general, the face and jaw should feel relaxed. There should be a "lifting" sensation in the cheeks. The lips must not be too tense either in the [i] or [u] postures.

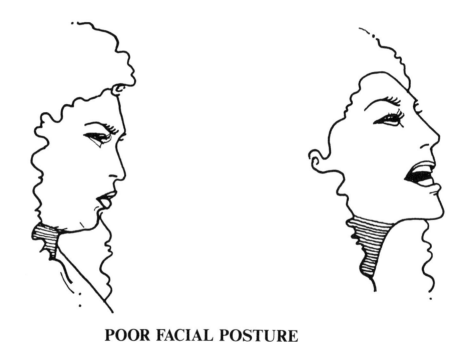

POOR FACIAL POSTURE

The inferior posture, primarily the tongue and soft palate positions, also are most important. Basic to all vowels are the following principles:

1. the soft palate always should be in a raised position when singing.

2. The height of the tongue (its midsection, not its tip) along with the position of the lips should be the primary focus of the developing singer when working on vowel production.

The Raised Soft Palate. The correct singing position of the inside of the mouth is the feeling of the beginning of a "yawn-sigh." The singer who has this sensation should also have a raised soft palate (velum) and an enlarged pharynx (back of the mouth). Be careful not to yawn fully. This will cause the swallowing muscles to tense, creating a strident sound. Be sure that the tip of the tongue touches the base of the bottom front teeth during all sustained vowel sounds.

Tongue/Lip Positions. The singer should approximate the following lip, and tongue positions for the three fundamental vowels.

Approximate positions of tongue, lips and oral pharynx when sung at medium pitch.

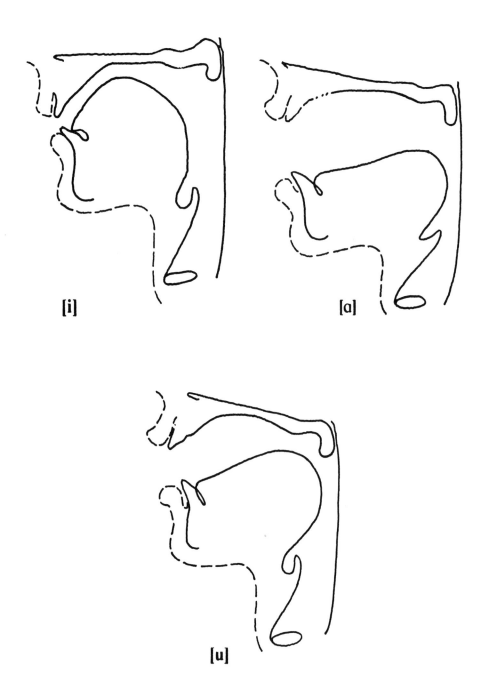

BEYOND THE FUNDAMENTAL VOWELS

By practicing Italian vowels the singer can learn to form the basic sounds for all languages while producing a resonant, pleasant tone. All other vowel sounds are modifications or combinations of these sounds. The basic vowels for singing are:

I.P.A. Symbol	English Word
[i]	see (ee) - fundamental vowel
[e]	chaotic (approximate sound; ay as in day but without the diphthong [i] or [I] sound at the end)
[ɛ]	wed (ed)
[ɑ]	father (ah) - fundamental vowel
[ɔ]	awful or off (aw)
[o]	obey (approximate sound; o as in go but without the diphthong [u] sound at the end)
[u]	noon (oo) - fundamental vowel

The Italian vowels may be placed in the three different "families" or postures, again based on the fundamental vowel positions. Slight changes will occur in tongue and jaw position as the singer moves from [u] to [o] to [ɔ] and from [ɑ] to [ɛ] to [e].

    I. [ɑ] family (posture)   [ɑ]
                                        [ɛ]
                                        [e]
   II. [i] family   [i]
 III. [u] family   [u]
                                        [o]
                                        [ɔ]

Note: In some instances the singer may form this vowel [e] more in the [i] posture. Care should then be taken not to cause undue tension in the jaw and at the root of the tongue.

When singing in English, the following postures are recommended. Again, the tongue will change (not the tip!), but in general the facial appearance stays the same.

    I. [ɑ]
      [e]
      [ɛ]
      [æ] apple   [ɑ] family
      [ʌ] up
      [ə] above
   II. [i]
      [I] it   [i] family
 III. [u]
      [o]
      [ɔ]
      [ʊ] should   [u] family
      [ɜ] learn

The English vowels [I], [æ], [ʌ], [ə], [ʊ], and [ɜ] often give the singer (and collectively a chorus) great difficulties. The sound is often unpleasant and only gets worse when a group of singers is asked to enunciate these vowels more clearly. If the singer will form the fundamental or "parent" vowel and say (tongue, sometimes lips change) the troublesome vowel, the tone is usually improved.

Examples:

[æ] in "happy"   Form [ɑ] (shape in pharynx and on face).
                        Say [æ] (only the tongue changes, not the tip but the sides).
                        Be careful not to sing "hoppy" instead of "happy"

18

[ʊ] in "full"   Form [ɑ] (shape in pharynx and on face, especially lips).
                       Say [ʊ] (Lips should open "North & South", not "East & West").
                       Be careful not to sing "fool" instead of "full".

Another problem area in English diction is the formation of diphthongs and triphthongs. Some choral directors have expressed the opinion that ninety percent of all choral difficulties in tuning, balance, blend, and tone quality could be greatly alleviated by attending to diphthongs. Listed below are five diphthongs and two triphthongs which need special attention:

I.P.A. Symbol	Sample Word
[ɑɪ]	light
[ɛɪ]	say
[ɔɪ]	toy
[ɑʊ]	how
[oʊ]	go
[ɑɪə]	fire
[ɑʊə]	our

The singer should sing on the first vowel of the diphthong or triphthong for almost the full value of the note. At the very end of the note, the second vowel is produced. Usually singers will tend to mix the two vowels from the very beginning. Awareness of and consistent practice in these areas will greatly improve the "choral sound".
Example:

light   [lɑ]   [I]   [t]

Pure vowels (as explained and discussed earlier) may be sung in lower and middle ranges of the voice. As the pitch ascends into the upper range, alterations of the vowels should be employed. Through the "break" areas (registration shifts) and into the higher notes, a general "rounding" and "lengthening" of the vowel should occur. When singing their highest pitches, singers may need to alter all vowels toward [ɑ] or [ʊ] to achieve more resonating space. This larger resonating space for higher notes will improve the sound, lessen vocal strain and fatigue, and help prevent vocal damage. The singer who tries to sing the same vowel sounds throughout his range will actually begin to lose clarity and tone color as he ascends in pitch. This is a very difficult notion for the inexperienced singer to accept; therefore, special attention and drill will be necessary and important.

CONSONANTS

While primary attention should be focussed on the vowels (soft palate and tongue/lip position), the consonants can not be neglected. Consonants are the noise that set the vowels apart when singing. They are not the pleasant, lovely sounds for which singers are known. They merely frame the vowels to make the text understandable. Most consonants, therefore, should be crisply produced, yet most English speakers tend to minimize or leave inaudible some consonants, overemphasize others, and harshly produce still others. Regional dialects again influence, usually improperly, the production of consonants.

The inexperienced singer must focus on two basic tasks with regard to consonants, other than the general attempts to speak each consonant clearly:
1. the proper musical distinction between "voiced and voiceless" or "unvoiced" consonants.
2. the proper production of the "problem" consonants.

Voiceless consonants are those that may be whispered or that merely are noise. Voiced consonants are those that require the vocal folds to be set in motion. For example, voiceless consonants include p, t, k, f, s; voiced consonants include m, n, v, z, j. To properly sing voiced consonants the singer must place the consonant on precisely the same pitch as the preceeding or following vowel. The inside of the mouth should be shaped as closely as possible to that which is proper for the preceeding or following vowel. Voiced consonants should be sung before the rhythmic beat so that the vowel falls on the beat. To properly produce voiceless consonants, the singer should place them in rhythmically accurate positions and should make them clear and short. All voiced and voiceless consonants should be properly pronounced and one should not be substituted for the other. For example: "I am waiting for you" is often pronounced "I am wading for you". "Please pray for me" often is lazily pronounced "Please bray for me".

Problem consonants each have their own solutions. Careful attention to production of the following consonants will help vocal quality.

[r]   1. Minimize the [r] before a consonant. Example: The Lord is good.
          2. Never sing [r] with back teeth close together.
          3. Do not sing [r] when it ends the phrase. Use the neutral vowel [ə] to finish the word. Example: I saw a shooting staə, not star.

[h]   This is an aspirate, a consonant which blows a puff of air through the vocal cords. If following vowel sounds are "breathy", work for a shorter, less lengthy [h].

[l]   1. When singing beginning l (1st letter of the word), keep the tongue forward and flip it down from the upper gum. Keep tongue independent from the jaw. Jaw should not move up and down when singing l's.
          2. Do not place an unnecessary vowel after [l] when it ends the phrase. Example: That is all (uh). [m] [n] [ng] These consonants demand a slightly lowered soft palate. Keep tongue forward, throat opened, and jaw relaxed. Be sure that the following vowel has a completely lifted soft palate.

[s]   1. Do not prolong the [s] sound. This causes an undesirable hissing noise in the chorus.
          2. When [s] divides a word, be sure to place it with the following syllable. Example: blessing

GOOD HEALTH AND CARE OF THE VOICE

Like physical hygiene, vocal hygiene is extremely important. For the singer two major enemies which produce unhealthy singing are lack of breath support and tension around the vocal mechanism. Loud, unsupported screaming at an atheletic event and loud, unsupported singing are both harmful to the voice and should be avoided. The instrumentalist can trade his or her cheaper model for a professional quality instrument when skill levels increase, but the singer only has one voice...forever. If it is cared for when young it will function properly for a long time, but, if abused, it will not. The voice must be protected by student and teacher.

The following are suggestions for keeping young voices healthy:

1. Follow general rules of good health.
2. Take care of allergies and respiratory diseases.
3. Keep the voice from becoming dehydrated:
   Drink plenty of water.
   Avoid an over dry atmosphere.
   Avoid antihistamines and other drying agents, if possible, and decrease vocal activities when using them.
4. Avoid tobacco and abusive drugs.
5. Learn and practice good speech habits:
   Avoid screaming and yelling.
   Do not talk constantly.
   Do not speak at a pitch too low or high for your singing voice.
6. Exercise the singing voice regularly.
7. Develop and practice good habits in these areas of vocal techniques: Posture, Breathing, Register, Resonance, and Diction.

MATERIALS OF MUSIC

SOUND

The world is full of sounds. Every day millions of people hear millions of different sounds: of birds, of wind, of running water, of laughter, of jet planes . . . the list is endless. Some sounds bring delight, while others are annoying. It is in this wonderful world of sound that the musician works. Composers and performers use sounds of various kinds and combinations to create music.

Sound is caused by vibration. The vibrations move through the air in a way that resembles waves in water. Each set of vibrations (or sound waves) has its own different shape and form. Many of these waves are familiar to us. For example, if two animals "sing" together—a bird and a human—one can easily identify each. They produce two different, yet familiar sounds. Each person creates a unique sound when speaking or singing because we all create unique sound waves.

WHAT IS SOUND?

How can we define sound? You can't touch it or see it. Nevertheless, there are ways that sound can be defined. Any sound has four basic elements that make it unique.

1. **Timbre.** (pronounced <u>tam</u> - ber) This means the basic identifying quality of any given sound. The timbre of a car horn is very different from a cat's meow. The vibrations each one makes are unique. Does a guitar sound like a church bell? No, because one has the timbre of a guitar and the other the timbre of a church bell. Things that are shaped differently, made from different materials, of different sizes, and struck differently create different vibrations. Somehow we learn to associate different sounds with the right sound source without ever even thinking about it.

2. **Duration.** The length of time that something lasts is its duration, and sounds have durations. A sound's duration can be very short or very long.

3. **Pitch.** A sound can be high or low. Think of the difference in pitch (how high or low a sound is) between a bird singing and a fog horn, or between a woman's voice and a man's voice. There are even sounds pitched so high or so low that we cannot hear them.

4. **Dynamic level.** The loudness or softness of a sound is called its dynamic level. A sound can be very soft or very loud, or anywhere in between those two extremes.

Listen to any sound. Does it have a unique timbre, or does it remind you of other sounds? How long does it last? Is it high or low? Soft or loud?

MUSICAL SOUNDS

The four basic sound ingredients—timbre, duration, pitch, dynamic level—can be used to describe basic ingredients of music as well. How do these relate to music?

1. **Timbre.** In music timbre means the type of sound that is created. A composer chooses what timbre is to be sounded by writing music for a certain instrument or a combination of instruments. For example, a piece of music written for chorus might be sung by a combination of sopranos, altos, tenors and basses. (The human voice is a shining example of a musical instrument.) A soprano section in a choir has a certain timbre. In fact, if we listened to every choir in the world we would find that every soprano section has a slightly

different timbre. Why? Because each soprano section in each choir is made up of a unique combination of unique, individual voices. That's why your choir will sound differently from any other choir in the world.

2. **Duration.** In music we call durations—how long a note is sounded—rhythms. Each note in a piece of music has a specific rhythm, a length of time it is to be held.

3. **Pitch.** A musical pitch is a note, be it a high note or a low note, or a note in the medium range. On a piano there are 88 notes or pitches. Your voice has a certain number of notes, from the lowest part of your voice to the highest.

4. **Dynamic level.** Is all music loud? Is all music soft? Of course not. Music is full of all sorts of contrasts. These contrasts in loudness and softness in music are called dynamics.

Try this experiment. Listen to any piece of music. As you listen try and hear the four ingredients of musical sound.

1. Listen for timbre. What instruments are playing, or what voices are singing? Can you identify the instruments? Listen for the timbre—the unique sound—of each instrument or voice.

2. Listen for durations, rhythms. Can you hear the difference between long notes and short notes? Can you hear any patterns in the rhythms?

3. Listen to the pitches. Can you hear the difference between high notes and low notes? Can you hear a pattern in the way the notes occur?

4. Listen for dynamics. Are there contrasts between loud and soft sections?

NOTATION

Notation simply means a way of writing something down. Musical notation is a way of writing down the basic ingredients of music: timbre, duration, pitch and dynamics.

Why do we need notation in music? Let's imagine that we would like to sing a piece of music composed by Johann Sebastian Bach. Bach lived over two hundred years ago. There were no systems of recording sounds in those days, no records or tapes. They didn't even have electricity then. So we can't listen to a recording of Bach's piece from two hundred years ago and learn it by imitating what we hear. Bach needed a way to write his music down on paper so that other people could perform his piece. And today we can sing a piece written over two hundred years ago because of musical notation. It was written on paper in a special language that tells us what notes to sing, what rhythms to sing, how loud to sing. Bach didn't have to invent this musical language. It had been developed hundreds of years before his time. But there was a time in human history when there was no language for writing music down on paper.

The ancient Greeks and Romans wrote letters of the alphabet in patterns that could be a reminder as to how a piece of music was to sound. But no one would have been able to read these patterns of letters without ever hearing the music and know what music to sing. At that time all music was learned by listening and copying what you heard. People had to memorize the tune for every song they wanted to know. There wasn't an adequate way of writing these tunes on paper.

In the early Christian church music was very important, just as it is in churches today. But like the Greeks and Romans before them, the early Christians had no system for writing music down. For hundreds of years the only way of learning music was to memorize what you heard other people sing. By the eighth century there were so many songs (or chants, as they were called in the early church) that it was impossible for the choirs to remember all of them. Something had to be invented to help people learn and remember music.

THE BEGINNINGS OF MUSICAL NOTATION

Around the year 800, over 1100 years ago, the monasteries were the center of all learning in Europe. Monks were the teachers of the time, whether it be teaching people to read or teaching people music. It was only natural that the monks would be the people who would invent ways of notating music.

They had been using a system of hand signals to help the choirs remember songs. A leader or teacher would stand in front of the choir and make motions with his hands to show the choir whether the melody was headed up or down. This wasn't specific enough to answer the problem of learning and remembering music, but it did provide the inspiration for the first written system devised by monks. They wrote on paper, above the words to the chants, markings that showed where the melody went. These markings were called *neumes*. At first they showed just the general shape of a melody, but gradually became more and more specific.

Around the year 950 the monks began using a horizontal line as a way of making the pitches of the melody of a song relate to one another in a more specific way. The single horizontal line represented the note F. The notes of the melody would be placed above or below the line (F) to indicate how high or low they were in relation to this central point of reference. A note just above F would be written slightly above the line, while a note much higher than F would be placed far above the line. The monks soon saw that if they added more lines, like the F line, they would have a clearer system. Gradually, more lines were added until centuries later there were 5 lines that were used as a standard point of reference for writing pitches. The spaces between the lines also referred to specific notes. Later in this book we will learn the details of how this written system of notation works.

MUSICAL NOTATION—AN INTERNATIONAL LANGUAGE

Musical notation is one of the world's great inventions. It is a language that communicates music across hundreds of years. By using a system of written music, musicians all over the world can learn the same music. It is the one language that people of all cultures can learn to understand and to use. And by learning to understand this language by learning to read music, you can become part of this international community. By learning to read music we can play or sing music written anywhere in the world, from music written hundreds of years ago to the latest compositions.

Learning to read music (understanding musical notation) is very much like learning to read the written English language. When you were a small child you learned the alphabet and how letters are combined to form words. You learned what different words mean, and how they are combined to make sentences. In this same manner, when we learn to read music, we learn what the basic tools of the language are and how they are combined. Believe it or not, you can learn to read a page of music as easily as you can read this page of the written English language!

THE STAFF AND CLEFS

The first basic tool in the language of music is the *staff*. A musical staff consists of five horizontal, parallel lines. Between these five lines there are four spaces.

What do the lines and spaces of a staff mean? We need another basic tool to tell us, something called a *clef*. Clefs come in several different varieties. Here are three of the most commonly used clefs.

THE TREBLE CLEF

The treble clef developed from a stylized capital G as a monk of many hundreds of years ago might have written it.

When we place the treble clef on a staff it makes the lines and spaces always mean specific notes.

If you remember that the nickname for the treble clef is the G clef, this will help you to remember what the lines and spaces mean. Look closely at the treble clef on the staff above. Notice how the curl in the middle of the symbol (not the curl on the bottom) wraps around the G line.

THE TENOR CLEF

While this clef is not as commonly used as the treble clef, it is occasionally used. It is called the tenor clef because in times past it was often used for writing the tenor part of music for chorus.

When we place the tenor clef on the staff, the lines and spaces mean different notes than with the treble clef. The tenor clef is sometimes called a C clef, simply because the middle of the clef symbol happens on the C line.

THE BASS CLEF

The bass clef (pronounced base) is the last clef we will introduce.

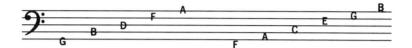

When the bass clef is placed on the staff, the lines and spaces mean different notes than a staff with the treble clef or the tenor clef. The bass clef is sometimes called the F clef. One reason is because many centuries ago a monk might have made a capital F like this when he was doing elaborate lettering. The more important reason is that the two dots of the bass clef surround the F line.

THE GRAND STAFF

If we use the treble clef and the bass clef together in the following manner we have the *grand staff*. The grand staff is the basis of how most music is written.

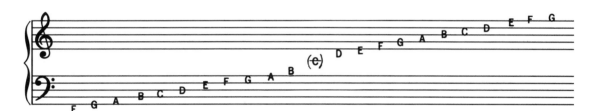

As you might guess from how this grand staff is written, the treble clef is used for higher notes, the bass clef for lower notes.

ADDING NOTES TO THE GRAND STAFF

There is a basic music tool that allows us to add notes to any clef. This is called a *ledger line*. By adding ledger lines we can write notes that are higher or lower than those on the staff. In the following example notice how adding a ledger line also automatically adds a space above and below the ledger line.

Remember, ledger lines are simply a way of temporarily extending a staff so that we can write notes that are higher or lower than can be written on the staff.

By using one ledger line in the following example we can write all the notes that exist from the bottom of the bass clef to the top of the treble clef. What is this combined system of treble clef and bass clef called? (The grand staff, of course.) To learn the language of music it is necessary to memorize the lines and spaces of the grand staff, just as years ago you memorized the alphabet when you were learning to read.

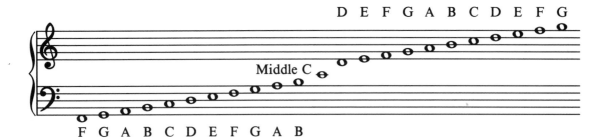

OCTAVES

Because many of us are familiar with the way a piano keyboard looks, we will use this to learn the next basic rule in music. On the piano moving to the right means going higher; moving to the left means going lower. Look at how the grand staff applies to the notes on the piano.

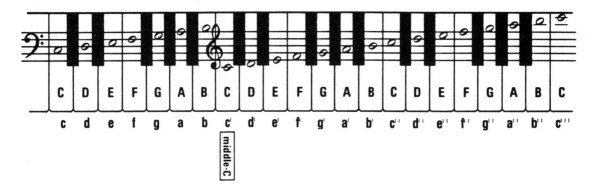

Have you noticed how in music we use the letters of the alphabet A through G? Why is it that when we get to G we start again with A? This is because of something magical in music called an *octave*. Look again at the piano keyboard above and find middle C. Starting with one on that note, count eight notes to the right or left. What do you find? You've come to another C, haven't you? We already know that moving to the right on the piano takes us higher, and moving to the left takes us lower. So we can conclude that while all the C's on the piano are the same basic pitch, that some are higher and some are lower. The distance between one C and the next C, higher or lower, is called an octave. If you were to go to the piano and find the notes on the chart, playing all the C's, you could easily hear that these are higher and lower versions of the same note.

Now you know why in music we start over with A after we get to the note G. It's because from A to A that magical sound, the octave happens.

SHARPS AND FLATS

Look once more at the diagram of the piano keyboard, this time noticing the black keys. As you can see, these notes are not labeled with either a line or space on the grand staff. But there is a way for us to write these notes.

A sharp sign in music looks like this: ♯. If we write a sharp sign before a note it means to play or sing the next highest note. On the piano diagram this would be the next note to the right. For instance, F sharp is the black note between F and G on the piano. On the grand staff this note is written like this:

F sharp

Any note on the staff can become a sharp note. Most of the time this will mean the black key to the right of it on the piano, but it could mean a white key. If we look at the piano diagram we can see that there is no black key between E and F, or between B and C. So E sharp would actually be another way of indicating F, and B sharp would be another way of indicating C.

There is another way that we write the "black notes" on the staff. A flat sign looks like this: ♭. If this sign appears before a note, it means to play or sing the next lowest note. On the piano, this would be the next note to the left. For instance, B flat is the note between B and A, the black note on the piano. On the grand staff this note is written like this:

B flat

Now that we know the basic tools of the grand staff, it's time to look at another and equally important area in the language of music—rhythm.

RHYTHM

Have you ever clapped along, or tapped your foot as music was being played? What is it that you were clapping or tapping? You were marking the beat of the music, or the pulse. All music has a pulse that keeps it going over a certain period of time until the music stops. Just as your heartbeat might speed up or slow down, the pulse in a piece of music might speed up or slow down. But it is always there. There may not always be a drummer who constantly plays the beat, but in all music there is a pulse, sometimes hardly perceptible.

This pulse is the basis for all musical rhythm. The rhythms in a piece of music are based on this everpresent pulse.

Let's try some rhythmic patterns over a beat. Your teacher will count to eight. His/her counting will be the pulse. On the chart below, clap on the X's and rest (silence) on the O's as your teacher says the numbers. It is very important that you feel the steady pulse that is being given.

	1	2	3	4	5	6	7	8	
	X	O	X	X	X	O	X	X	(REPEAT)

Try these other patterns in the same manner. Are you able to feel the pulse?

	1	2	3	4	5	6	7	8
a.	X	O	X	X	X	O	X	X
b.	X	O	O	X	X	O	O	X
c.	X	O	O	X	O	O	X	X
d.	O	X	O	X	O	X	O	X
e.	X	O	O	O	O	O	O	X

NOTES AND RESTS

In the language of written music there are several different ways that notes are written that tell us how many beats the note is held. The chart below explains the basic types of notes.

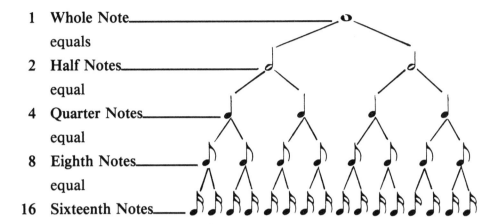

1   Whole Note

equals

2   Half Notes

equal

4   Quarter Notes

equal

8   Eighth Notes

equal

16   Sixteenth Notes

There are also symbols in music for telling us how many beats we should rest, or remain silent. The chart below explains the basic types of rests. Notice how they correspond with the note chart above.

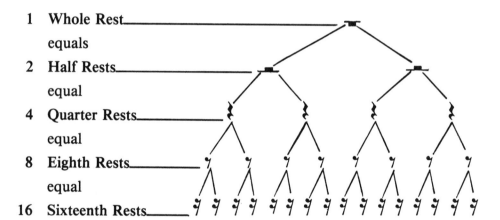

1   Whole Rest

equals

2   Half Rests

equal

4   Quarter Rests

equal

8   Eighth Rests

equal

16   Sixteenth Rests

METER

The ongoing pulse of a piece of music is divided into small sections called *measures* or *bars*. The meter of a piece of music tells us how many beats are in each measure, and what note equals one beat. There are always two numbers on each clef to show the meter, one on top of the other, looking like this:

The top number of the metrical marking (another way to refer to the meter) tells us how many beats are in each measure. In this case there are four beats per measure. The bottom number of the metrical marking tells us which note equals one beat. The 4 in the lower position refers to the quarter note. So in the example above there would be four quarter notes for each measure.

If we know which note gets one beat, we can easily figure out the value of the other types of notes. It's a simple mathematical formula. (Did you know that math plays a very important role in music?) If the meter is $\frac{4}{4}$ (4 beats to a measure, 1 beat per quarter note), the other note values would be:

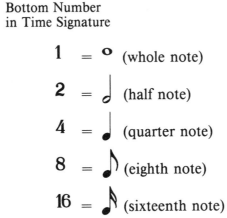

Another name for the meter of a piece of music is its *time signature*. The bottom number of the time signature is a short way of referring to different types of notes. The chart below explains what note the bottom number of the time signature refers to:

Bottom Number
in Time Signature

1 = o (whole note)

2 = 𝅗𝅥 (half note)

4 = ♩ (quarter note)

8 = ♪ (eighth note)

16 = 𝅘𝅥𝅯 (sixteenth note)

The time signature of a piece not only refers to the note values, but also to the rest values. In a time signature of $\frac{4}{4}$ we already know that there are 4 beats per measure and that the quarter note equals one beat. The quarter rest also equals one beat with this time signature. The chart below illustrates the value of the rests in $\frac{4}{4}$ time.

$$\blacksquare = 4 \text{ beats (whole rest)}$$

$$\blacksquare = 2 \text{ beats (half rest)}$$

$$\frac{4}{4} \quad \xi = 1 \text{ beat (quarter rest)}$$

$$\gamma = \tfrac{1}{2} \text{ beat (eighth rest)}$$

$$\gamma = \tfrac{1}{4} \text{ beat (sixteenth rest)}$$

There are three time signatures illustrated below, along with the note and rest values for each.

$\frac{4}{4}$		$\frac{2}{4}$		$\frac{2}{2}$	
$\circ$, $\blacksquare$ = 4 beats		$\circ$, $\blacksquare$ = 2 beats		$\circ$, $\blacksquare$ = 2 beats	
$\downarrow$, $\blacksquare$ = 2 beats		$\downarrow$, ξ = 1 beat		$\circ$, $\blacksquare$ = 1 beat	
$\downarrow$, ξ = 1 beat		$\flat$, γ = ½ beat		$\downarrow$, ξ = ½ beat	
$\flat$, γ = ½ beat		$\flat$, γ = ¼ beat		$\flat$, γ = ¼ beat	
$\flat$, γ = ¼ beat					

If we place a dot after a note or rest it automatically becomes 1½ times its normal value. If a quarter note equals one beat, then a dotted quarter note equals one and one half beats. If a half note equals two beats, then a dotted half note equals 3 beats. With this in mind, we can understand the following chart.

$$\circ \cdot = \downarrow \downarrow \downarrow \qquad \downarrow \cdot = \downarrow \downarrow \downarrow \qquad \downarrow \cdot = \flat \flat \flat \qquad \flat \cdot = \flat \flat \flat$$

Dotted Whole Note   Dotted Half Note   Dotted Quarter Note   Dotted Eighth Note

Knowing about dotted rhythms allows us to create time signature charts that show all the major variations of note and rest values.

Clap the following rhythmic patterns as your teacher beats a steady pulse. Before beginning each example ask yourself: 1) How many beats per measure? and 2) What note equals one beat?

TIES

A musical tie is a curved line drawn between two notes on the same pitch.

If a note is tied to another note, then the note is held through the value of the second note. The second note is not repeated. In $\frac{4}{4}$ time, a half note tied to a quarter note would be held a total of 3 beats. In the same time signature, an eighth note tied to a quarter note would be held a total of 1½ beats. Clap the following examples as your teacher keeps a steady beat. Remember, do not repeat tied notes.

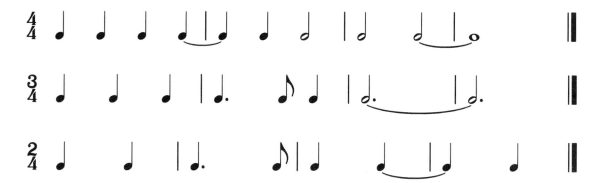

TRIPLETS

By now we know that 2 eighth notes equal one quarter note, and that 4 sixteenth notes equal one quarter note. But there is a way of writing three even notes that will equal one quarter note. This is done by using a *triplet*. This grouping of three notes usually has the number "3" above or below it, making it very easy to identify it as a triplet.

There are other varieties of triplets, but for now let's study only the type of triplet where the quarter note is divided into three equal notes. Clap the following examples as your teacher keeps a steady beat.

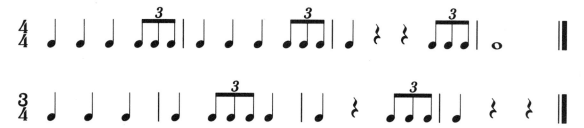

FURTHER DETAILS ABOUT NOTES

The parts of the written musical notes all have names, and each has a standard way that it should be written on the page. Examine the chart below.

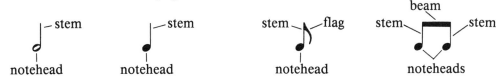

STEPPING UP TO THE SCALES

Let's look once more at the diagram of the staff as it applies to the piano.

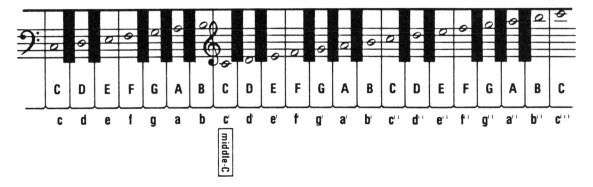

The distance between one note and the very next note, be it a black note or a white note, is called a half step. Two half steps make what we call a whole step. These two intervals are the basic building blocks for the notes in any musical melody. An interval is the distance between one note and another note.

If we combine whole steps and half steps in certain patterns we can build musical scales. Scales are important because so much of our music is based on them.

MAJOR SCALES

The following pattern of whole steps and half steps gives us a *major scale*, no matter which note we use to begin the scale. A major scale consists of eight notes, and we will use numbers from one through eight to name the notes.

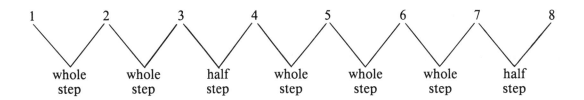

Using the piano as a point of reference, this scale looks like this on the treble clef. Besides using numbers, there are syllables that are used for each note of the scale, shown below.

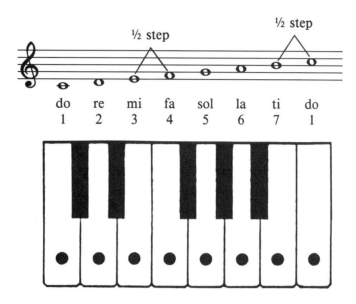

Remember, a major scale can begin on any note, so for a major scale beginning on D, then D would be *do,* E would be *re,* F♯ would be *mi,* etc. If we begin a major scale on G, then G is *do,* A is *re,* etc. The chart below illustrates several major scales with the proper syllables. Can you find the half steps and the whole steps on the keyboard?

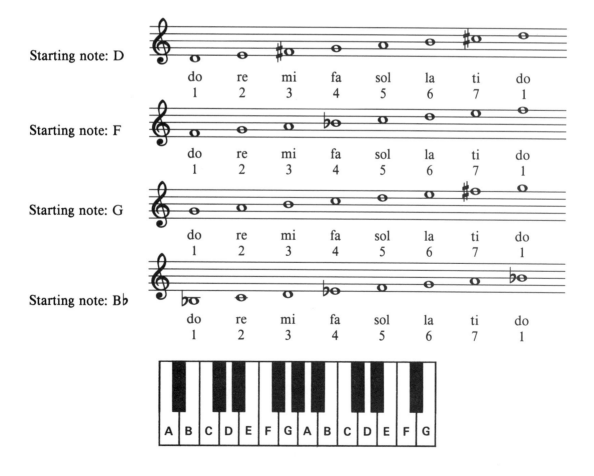

MINOR SCALES

There is a type of scale other than the major scale called the *minor scale.* As you might guess, there is a different pattern of whole steps and half steps that are used to create a minor scale. In fact, there are three different types of minor scales, each one with a different pattern of notes. They all have one very important thing in common; all three minor scales begin on la.

1. **The Natural Minor Scale.**

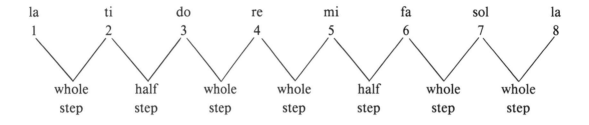

Using the piano as a point of reference, a natural minor scale beginning on A would look like this:

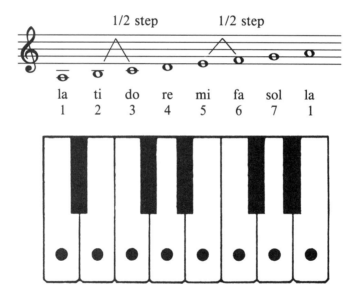

2. **The Harmonic Minor Scale.** When we raise one of the degrees of the scale by a half step the name of the syllable changes. For instance, in the harmonic minor scale below notice how sol becomes si. Those intervals not marked are all whole steps.

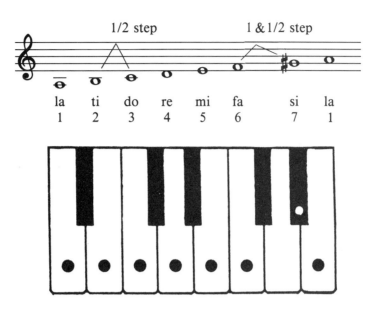

3. **The Melodic Minor Scale.** This scale is sung with one pattern going up and another going down. Notice how the notes *fa* and *sol* are raised one half step. The syllables then become *fi* and *si,* as indicted below.

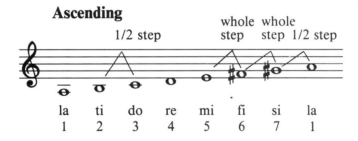

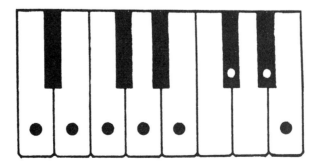

Descending

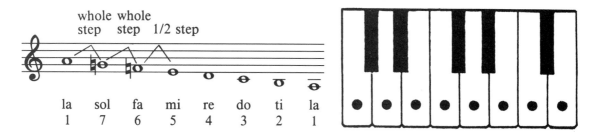

whole	whole	
step	step	1/2 step

la sol fa mi re do ti la
1 7 6 5 4 3 2 1

♮ = a natural sign.
This cancels out a sharp
or flat that was sung
previously (as in the
ascending scale)

THE CHROMATIC SCALE

If we start on C and count by half steps up to the next C, we find that there are twelve half steps in an octave. If we sing each of these half steps we are singing a chromatic scale. When going up, the normal syllables of the scale are modified each to end in *i* (pronounced ee) for the chromatic notes (the notes between the tones of the major scale.)

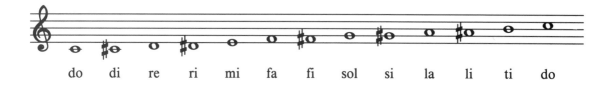

do di re ri mi fa fi sol si la li ti do

When going down, the normal scale tones are each modified to end in *e* (pronounced ay), except *re,* which is modified to *ra.*

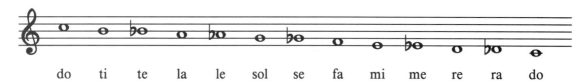

do ti te la le sol se fa mi me re ra do

A chromatic scale can begin with *do* on any note.

KEY SIGNATURES

A great deal of music is written based on the notes of a major or minor scale. The first note of a scale could be called the home note, or the key note. It's the most important note in the scale, because it's the note on which the scale is built. If we sing a piece of music that is based on the C major scale, then C is the key note, and we call it being in the key of C major. Another name for the home key is the *tonic* pitch. For example, the tonic of D major is D.

In many keys there are sharps and flats in the notes of the scale. You've already seen these in the section on the scales. If a piece of music is based on a scale, and that scale has sharps or flats in it, there is a convenient way that we can label all the sharps or flats at the beginning of the piece, rather than labeling each one as it occurs. This is called a *key signature*. A key signature, then, tells us what the home key of the music is, and tells us what sharps or flats to use. The following chart gives the key signatures for all the sharp keys. Notice how a major and a minor key use the same key signature, because the scales of the two related keys are built on the same notes. A minor scale can be built beginning on la of any major scale. A major scale and a minor scale that share the same key signature and scale tones are called relatives, simply because they are related. For instance, B minor is the relative minor of D major.

40

major (do) scale pattern   minor (la) scale pattern   key signature for
                                                                    relative maj. & min.

do re mi fa sol la ti do   la ti do re mi fa sol la   C maj.   A min.
1 2 3 4 5   6 7 1   1 2 3 4 5 6   7 1

do   la   G maj.   E min.

do   la   D maj.   B min.

do   la   A maj.   F♯ min.

do   la   E maj.   C♯ min.

do   la   B maj.   G♯ min.

do   la   C♯ maj.   A♯ min.

do   la   F♯ maj.   D♯ min.

The family of flat keys is given on a similar chart below.

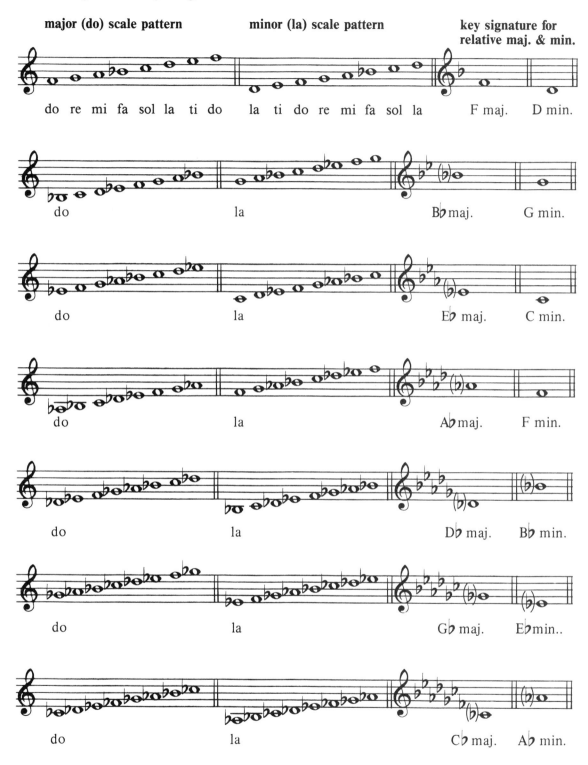

TEMPO MARKINGS

The speed of the beat through time is the *tempo*. It may be regular or irregular, slow or fast. It may change by slowing or quickening, suddenly or gradually. All these changes require symbols or instructions on the score (written music). The following are common markings regarding tempo.

very slow	slow	*moderate	fast	very fast
largo lento	andante	*moderato	allegro	vivace
grave	adagio	andantino	allegretto	presto

Moderato serves as a good reference tempo since it can be referred to as one's normal walking pace.

Additional terms referring to tempo:

a tempo —return to original tempo
accelerando —go faster; accelerate
allargando —slowing down, usually accompanied by a crescendo
rallentando —gradually slackening in speed
ritardando —gradually slackening in speed
rubato —a certain flexibility of tempo consisting of slight *ritards* and *accelerandos* alternating according to the requirements of musical expression
con moto —with motion
poco più mosso —a little more motion

In 1816, Johannes Maelzel invented the metronome, a mechanical instrument which could click regular beats. It featured a scale which allowed the user to set the number of clicks per minute. Beethoven first used the metronome's units to indicate the tempo for his compositions. Since that time the device has been used as a common indicator of tempo.

Common markings referring to metronomes:

1) **Circa (c. or ca.)**—approximately or about

2) **M.M. (or M)**—Maelzel's metronome (or metronome)

3) **M.M. ♩ = 60**—Maelzel's metronome—60 quarter notes per minute

4) **M ♩ = 44**—Metronome—44 half notes per minute

5) **♩ = 68**—68 quarter notes per minute

6) **♩ c. 120**—approximately 120 quarter notes per minute

MUSICAL DYNAMICS

It was not until relatively late in music's history that the need for markings for loudness or softness of music were needed. Today we use the following symbols to indicate dynamic level.

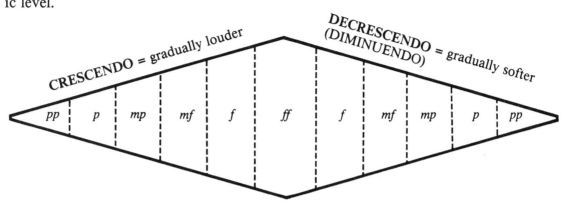

pp —**pianissimo** = very soft

p —**piano** = soft

mp —**mezzo piano** = medium soft

mf —**mezzo forte** = medium loud

f —**forte** = loud

ff —**fortissimo** = very loud

= sing gradually louder

= sing gradually softer

MUSICAL SYMBOLS

In addition to tempo and general dynamic markings, there are special markings that are used in music to indicate specific things, sometimes just involving one note. The following is a brief list of those musical symbols encountered most often.

The dots under the notes are called *staccato* markings. These mean the notes should be played or sung in a very short, detached manner. The opposite of staccato is *legato,* meaning smoothly.

Notes marked in this manner should be slightly stressed, and played legato.

These are heavy accents. Notes marked in this manner should be strongly punched and brought out.

This is the next heaviest accent. The notes so marked should be stressed more than a normal note would be, but not necessarily punched in a strong manner.

This is a *fermata*. It means to hold this note much longer than the rhythm of the note would indicate.

Repeat signs, such as these, tell us to sing or play the enclosed music again.

D.S. al Coda ⊕

This means to return to the special sign (𝄋) and continue until the sign that takes us to the coda. This sign looks like this: ⊕, and is sometimes accompanied by the words "to coda". A coda is a section of music at the end of the piece, and is marked as being the "Coda".

MUSICAL FORM

All art has form. This is easy to see when we look at a sculpture. It has a particular shape that is plain to everyone. And if we know a little bit about art, or have a teacher to guide us, we can look at a sculpture and find patterns in the shape, the proportions of different sections of the sculpture, and balance in the design. Perhaps you've never thought of it like this, but music has form too. In fact, just as sculpture is carved out in material and takes its form in a space, music is carved out in sound and takes its form over a period of time. We could think of music as a sculpture in time.

Think of your school building. It's a piece of architecture, of course, and it definitely has form. We could see this form from many different angles. If we walked around your school we would notice different things about the building from every point of view. If we stand across the street we can see the large shape of the building, or at least one side of it, better than we can if we are standing right in front of it. And if we stand very close we can probably see small details that we couldn't see from farther away. If we walk through the building, we get an entirely different view of the form. And if we were to fly high above it in a plane or a helicopter we would see yet another view of your school.

So you see, looking at the form of something can mean many things, depending on your point of view. Just as we can't see the entire form of your school from any one point, we can't hear everything about a piece of music in any one splice of it. We have to let it unfold and hear the entire piece to grasp the form. And even then, we can't listen to all the details with one hearing. If we want to study a piece of music, examining how it's put together, we might need to hear it many times, as well as studying the printed score.

Every piece of music has a unique form. It might be on a very large scale, such as a symphony, or on a very small scale, such as a short, simple song. But there is a fundamental building block to the form of all music called a *phrase.* Think of a story you've read, and how each sentence joins together to make a paragraph. The paragraphs flow from one to another to tell the story. It may even be in larger sections, such as chapters. It's similar to how music is built. The phrases join together to make sections, and the sections join together to make the piece. The composer builds his or her phrases carefully so that the end result is a piece of music that holds together and has unity.

Let's look at a familiar song, "America the Beautiful." As you can see, the phrases have been labeled for you. As you sing through the song can you hear where each phrase begins and ends?

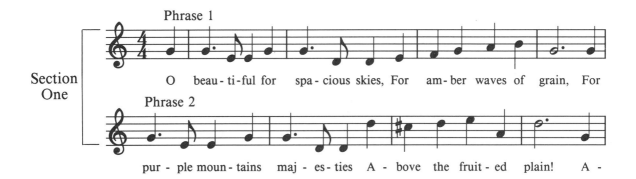

46

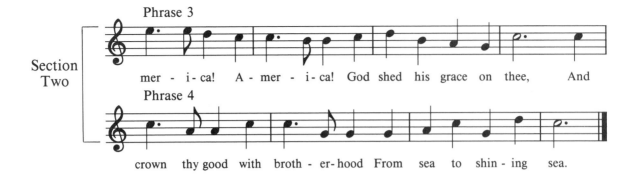

Section Two

Phrase 3

mer - i - ca! A - mer - i - ca! God shed his grace on thee, And

Phrase 4

crown thy good with broth - er-hood From sea to shin - ing sea.

Doesn't it seem as if the song is in two large sections? Section one is made up of phrases one and two. Both of these phrases begin with the same notes, but end differently. Still, they sound similar enough that we can easily think of them as one section. Section two consists of phrases three and four. While they do not begin the same, as did phrases one and two, they sound similar, don't they?

There is one more thing that we can notice about the phrases of this song. Look closely at the rhythm of each phrase, comparing each to the others. Have you noticed how each phrase has the same rhythm?

This rhythmic similarity gives the song a unity. It makes the song sound very satisfying, and makes each phrase seem a natural result of the one before it.

The combination of an identifying rhythm and a snatch of melody can be called a theme or a motive. This is well illustrated in the first two phrases of "America the Beautiful." The first two measures of each phrase could be called a motive. The third phrase is similar to the first two, not in notes, but in rhythm. The rhythm of the first two phrases seems to motivate the way the third phrase is built. The fourth phrase is similar to phrases one and two in both notes and rhythms; the motive is certainly at work here.

There is one more telltale sign of a musical phrase. Notice how each phrase ends on a longer held note, a dotted half note to be specific. When you sing the song, doesn't it seem as if each phrase comes to a natural resting point here? This is called the cadence of the phrase. Cadences are like punctuation in the written English language. Not all punctuation marks are the end of a sentence, and not all musical cadences are the end of a complete musical idea. Sing the first section again of "America the Beautiful." Notice how the cadence of the second phrase doesn't really sound like the end of the music. It sounds as if it's simply pausing before moving on to the next phrase, doesn't it? Now sing section two again. It is only the cadence of the last phrase that sounds as if we've come to the end of the music, the final cadence.

FINDING THE MUSICAL FORM

There is some music that is clearly written in defined sections. "Blow The Candle Out" is a song with three verses. Each verse has different words, but sung to the same music. The technical word for the type of form is *strophic*. The verse is made up of four musical phrases. Phrases 1 and 2 are the same music. Phrase 3 is a different musical idea. Phrase 4 is basically the same as phrases 1 and 2. This type of form is among the simplest designs for a piece of music.

Verse 1 is sung by the tenors and basses in unison. Verse 2 is sung by the sopranos and altos in unison. Verse 3 is sung by all parts in harmony.

Blow The Candles Out
For Four-Part Chorus of Mixed Voices
a cappella

Traditional   Arranged by Gregg Smith

48

Verse 2
Phrase 1

Phrase 3

can - not rest_ con - tent - ed while you are far a - way. The

can - not rest_ con - tent - ed while you are far a - way. The

Phrase 4

winds, they are so cold that we can - not stay there - out! So

winds, they are so cold that we can - not stay there - out! So

Phrase 3

hug-gin' one an - oth - er, so why not you and I. A-

hug-gin' one an - oth - er, so why not you and I. A-

hug-gin' one an - oth - er, so why not you and I. A-

hug-gin' one an - oth - er, so why not you and I. A-

Phrase 4

hug-gin' one an - oth - er, with - out a fear or doubt. So

hug-gin' one an - oth - er, with - out a fear or doubt. So

hug-gin' one an - oth - er, with - out a fear or doubt. So

hug-gin' one an - oth - er, with - out a fear or doubt. So

Let's look at the following song, "Away to Rio!", for the structural sections of the music.

Away To Rio!

Traditional Sea Chantey

Arranged by
Marshall Bartholomew

So that we can easily see what is going on, the measures have all been numbered, and we'll use these measure numbers as a point of reference. First, do you notice that the very first two notes of the song are in an incomplete measure? These are called pick up notes. Pick up notes are allowed at the beginning of a song. They lead us to beat one of the first complete measure, marked measure 1. Phrase one of this song is made up of measures 1-4. We can also see that this first phrase is in two smaller parts, part one being measures 1 and 2, part two being measures 3 and 4. Phrase two is measures 5-8, again made up of two smaller parts. Part one of phrase two is measures 5-6 (including the pick up note to measure 5), and part two is measures 7-8. Phrases one and two combined make what we will call section A. If you were to sing this song, or if your teacher plays it for you, you could hear how phrase two seems to be an answer to phrase one.

Measures 9-12 are phrase three (including the two eighth notes that are a pick up to measure 9). Notice how the basses sing the same notes in measures 9-10 as are sung in measures 11-12. If we compare the tenor part at the same point, we find that while the same notes are not repeated in measures 11-12 as were sung in measures 9-10, the melody has the same shape and rhythm. Phrase four runs from measures 13-16 (including the pick up note to measure 13). Phrases three and four combined make what we will call section B. You might also notice that on the music this is labeled "Refrain." Did you see the repeat sign in measure 16^1? It tells us to go back to measure 9 and sing the refrain a second time. The second time through the refrain we go from measure 15 to 16^2, skipping measure 16^1. Measure 16^1 is called a first ending; measure 16^2 is called a second ending. This is very commonly used in music where repeat signs occur.

So what do we wind up with? We have a section A (phrases one and two). We have a section B (phrases three and four). And we also repeat section B, taking the second ending on the repeat. One short way, then, to refer to the form of "Away to Rio!" would be ABB. The letters refer to the sections of the music and the order that they are given.

There is one more interesting thing that we can learn about the form of this song. Did you see that there are two lines of words in section A? When different words are sung to the same music in a section such as this we call them verses. "Away to Rio!" has two verses. When do we sing the second verse? We sing through the first verse, sing the refrain and repeat it, and then we go back to the beginning of the song and sing the second verse. After the second verse, we again sing the refrain and repeat it, so we wind up singing the ABB form twice through. The refrain of a song usually follows the verses. While verses often have different words each time through, the refrain most often has the same words every time it is sung.

What have we done? We've analysed this song, just like you might analyse a math problem or a science formula. Perhaps you've never realised it, but music can be dissected in this scientific manner. It can allow us to understand a song much more thoroughly, and will make singing a song more interesting if we look for these kinds of details. And it will help us memorize music, too!

To summarize what we've found out about "Away to Rio!" the following chart can be constructed.

Verse 1:	phrase 1, measures 1-4 phrase 2, measures 5-8	section A
Refrain:	phrase 3, measures 9-12 phrase 4, measures 13-16^1	section B
	repeat	
	phrase 3, measures 9-12 phrase 4, measures 13-16^2	section B

| Verse 2: | phrase 1, measures 1-4 | |
| | phrase 2, measures 5-8 | section A |

| Refrain: | phrase 3, measures 9-12 | |
| | phrase 4, measures 13-16[1] | section B |

| | repeat | |

| | phrase 3, measures 9-12 | |
| | phrase 4, measures 13-16[2] | section B |

Let's turn now to another song, looking for the form of the music. Again, the measures, phrases and sections have been labeled to help us see the structure of the piece.

TIME
For Three-Part Chorus of Treble Voices
with Piano Accompaniment

Inscription on Grandfather Clock
Chester Cathedral, England

DONNA GARTMAN SCHULTZ

58

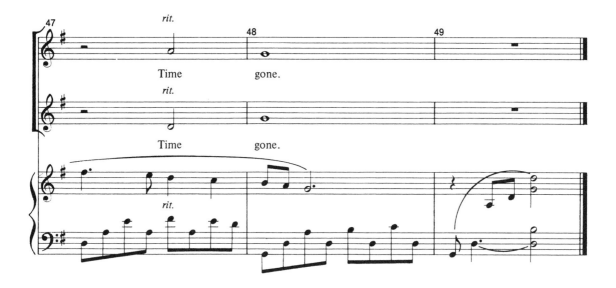

We can quickly get an overview of the form of this song if we're aware of looking for sections. The first thing that we always look for when searching for structure in music is a repeat of a section of music. Keep that in mind as we look at "Time".

Measures 1-4 are what is called an introduction. A great deal of music has a short section such as this to introduce the piece. You are certainly accustomed to hearing an introduction in lots of the choral music that you have sung.

Measures 5-21 are section A. How do we know that? If we sing this section we can easily hear that it is not until measure 21 that the music seems to come to a point of final punctuation, a period. The individual phrases that make up this large section all seem to be part of a whole, and at no point before measure 21 could we feel as if the music was coming to a definite final cadence. On the summary chart below the phrases of the section are spelled out specifically.

The piano plays an interlude beginning in measure 22, continuing through measure 25. An interlude in music is a short section that serves as a bridge between two larger sections.

Look at measure 26. You'll notice that the soprano part is exactly the same as in measure 5. And except for one small change (in measure 37) the soprano part in measures 26-41 is the same as in measures 5-21. That should tip us off right away that this is an important feature of the structure of this song. If we look closely at the piano part, comparing measures 5-21 and measures 26-41, we will notice that they are very, very similar. In fact, the only significant difference between measures 5-21 and measures 26-41 is that in the latter section there is an alto part added. If we sing the soprano part and the alto part together it becomes clear that the alto part is a harmony part, a counter melody to the soprano part. This is a common feature of music. Often when a section of music is repeated it is made different in some way. Adding the alto part the second time through is far more fun and interesting than if measures 5-21 had simply just been sung again.

Measures 42 and 43 are another brief interlude in the piano part, another bridge to a new section. Measures 44-49 are a final section that ends the piece. This type of section is sometimes called a coda. Often times the music of the coda is based on music that was heard previously. Look at the soprano part in measures 34 and 35. Now look at the soprano part in measures 44 and 45. They are the same notes, aren't they? The coda of a piece usually takes familiar material and uses it in a way that makes the ending seem final. Did you also notice that at the coda the chorus is divided into three parts for the first time in the piece? It simply is more dramatic, a better design for this song, to start with unison singing in the first section, two part singing in the second section, and three part singing at the coda. Can you see how natural and satisfying that design is? The coda is even made more dramatic by having the tempo slow down here. This is a common feature for the final section of music. Often times at or near the end the tempo will slow down, as if the piece is winding down.

The overview of the form of "Time" could be explained by saying that we have a section A that is repeated, with a coda at the end. The chart below gives a complete view of what we've discussed.

Introduction:	measures 1-4	
Section A:	measures 5-21	phrase 1, measures 5-8 phrase 2, measures 9-12 phrase 3, measures 13-17 phrase 4, measures 18-21
Interlude:	measures 22-25	
Section A, repeated:	measures 26-41	phrase 1, measures 26-29 phrase 2, measures 30-33 phrase 3, measures 34-37 phrase 4, measures 38-41
Interlude:	measures 42-43	
Coda:	measures 44-49	

64

We'll look at one more piece for form and structure.

Lullaby
For Unison Chorus of Young Voices
with Piano Accompaniment

from: Sing Song
by Christina Rossetti

Paul Hendrickson

Phrase B

Theme

Stars are up, the moon is peep - ing. Lul - la - by,

Phrase C

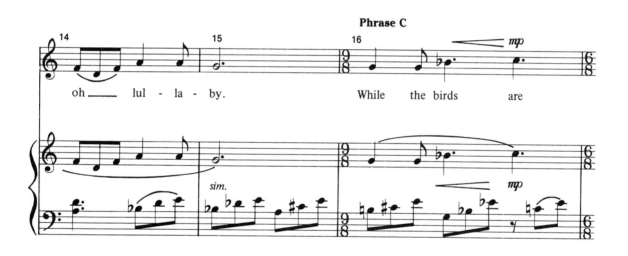

oh ___ lul - la - by. While the birds are

Theme

si - lence keep - ing. Lul - la - by,

Phrase D

Variation on the theme

Final Cadence

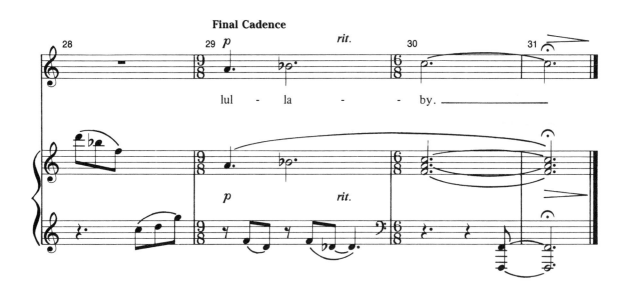

Not all music can be divided into sections as easily as "Away to Rio!" and "Time". There aren't large sections in "Lullaby" that are repeated to give us clues to the structure. Nevertheless, there is form to this music. Look at measures 3-5. Can you find this phrase again in the song? It occurs again at measures 8-10, 13-15, and 19-21. That's our first major clue to the structure, this repeated phrase.

Now look at the measures between this recurring phrase. Look at measures 6-7, 11-12, 16-18, and 22-24. Do we find repeated music? No. However, if we compare measures 6-8 and measures 22-24 we find that the shape of the line and the notes are very similar, even though the rhythm and words are different. This is a commonly found unifying device in music. Although the music isn't exactly repeated, measures 22-24 remind us of measures 6-7. But what about the other, different phrases? If we look closely we can find one similarity between these. They all end with a slowing or pause in the tempo. They all end with a ritardando or a fermata, don't they? So while they are dissimilar in most ways, they each have the same type of musical feel to them.

"Lullaby" is a good illustration of how a composer can take one short idea and make that the unifying element in the design of a song. Look at the chart below to see specifically how this works in this piece. We will call the music that is repeated, first appearing in measures 3-5, the theme.

Introduction:	measures 1-2
Theme:	measures 3-5
Phrase A:	measures 6-7
Theme:	measures 8-10
Phrase B:	measures 11-12
Theme:	measures 13-15
Phrase C:	measures 16-18
Theme:	measures 19-21
Phrase D:	measures 22-24
Variation on the theme:	measures 25-28
Final cadence:	measures 29-31

This type of musical form is one where the theme returns, but between theme statements there is new material. The name for this type of form is a *rondo*. This example is a very simple kind of rondo. Rondos can be as long and complex as a movement of a symphony.

In summary, we've seen two important facets of looking for form in music. We look for phrases, and how the phrases combine to make larger sections. Or if we do not find that the phrases build into a larger section, we look for how material is repeated. This is just the tip of the iceberg. There are endless mysteries to discover in studying the design of how music is put together. As you learn more about music, and become more perceptive a listener, you will begin to hear things beyond these two basic principles. The better we grasp the form of a piece of music, the more we can understand it. It takes a shape in the mind and in the memory.

SIGHT SINGING

When we learn to sight read, we can sing music that we've never even heard. If we know how to sing each interval (the distance between two notes), we can sing any melody by piecing these intervals together. As your teacher guides you through the exercises, keep in mind the following pointers for successful sight singing.

Sight Singing Pointers

1. Always look at the clef sign.

2. Sight singing not only means singing the correct notes. It also means singing the correct rhythms.

3. Look at the key signature to notice which notes are sharps and flats.

4. Always try and keep a steady beat. It's better to sing slowly and steadily than to disrupt the beat by speeding through some sections and stumbling through others.

5. Practice makes perfect!

PROGRESSIVE SIGHT SINGING EXERCISES

Featured Interval in exercises 1-3: Major 2nd (whole step)

examples:

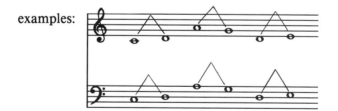

1. Key: C major.

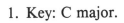

do re mi fa sol la ti do
1 2 3 4 5 6 7 1

do re mi   mi re do   do re mi re   do
1   2   3   3   2   1   1   2   3   2   1

2. Key: G major

do re mi fa sol la ti do
1 2 3 4 5 6 7 1

do re mi   mi re do   do re mi re   do
1   2   3   3   2   1   1   2   3   2   1

3. Key: F major

do re mi fa sol la ti do
1 2 3 4 5 6 7 1

do re mi re   mi re re do
1   2   3   2   3   2   2   1

Featured Interval in exercises 4-6: Major 3rd

examples:

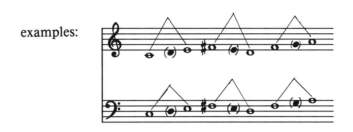

4. Key: C major

5. Key: F major

6. Key: D major

Featured Interval in exercises 7-9: minor 3rd

examples:

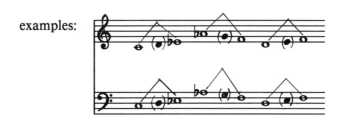

7. Key: C minor

la ti do re mi fa sol la
1　2　3　4　5　6　7　1

la ti do　ti do la　do la do ti　la do la
1　2　3　　2　3　1　　3　1　3　2　　1　3　1

8. Key: F major

do re mi fa sol la ti do
1　2　3　4　5　6　7　1

mi fa sol mi sol fa sol mi　sol　mi　sol
3　4　5　3　5　4　5　3　　5　　3　　5

9. Key: D minor

la ti do re mi fa sol la
1　2　3　4　5　6　7　1

la ti do la do ti do la　do ti　la
1　2　3　1　3　2　3　1　　3　2　　1

Featured Interval in exercise 10-12: Perfect 4th

examples:

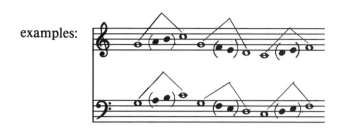

10. Key: G major

do re mi fa do fa mi re do re mi re do
1 2 3 4 1 4 3 2 1 2 3 2 1

11. Key: C minor

mi la sol sol fa mi la mi la mi la
5 1 7 7 6 5 1 5 1 5 1

12. Key: B♭ major

sol do sol do sol do ti la sol la ti do sol do
5 1 5 1 5 1 7 6 5 6 7 1 5 1

74

Featured Interval in exercises 13-15: Perfect 5th

examples:

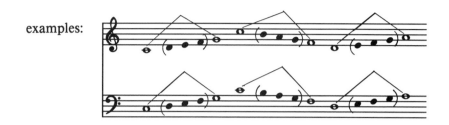

13. Key: C major

do	re	mi	fa	sol	la	ti	do
1	2	3	4	5	6	7	1

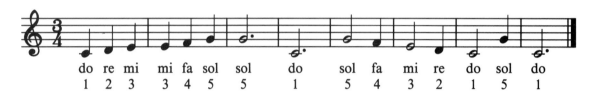

do	re	mi	mi	fa	sol	sol	do	sol	fa	mi	re	do	sol	do
1	2	3	3	4	5	5	1	5	4	3	2	1	5	1

14. Key: F minor

la	ti	do	re	mi	fa	sol	la
1	2	3	4	5	6	7	1

la	ti	do	la	mi	la	mi	do	re	ti	la	mi	la
1	2	3	1	5	1	5	3	4	2	1	5	1

15. Key: E minor

la	ti	do	re	mi	fa	sol	la
1	2	3	4	5	6	7	1

la	mi	la	mi	la	mi	mi	re	do	ti	la
1	5	1	5	1	5	5	4	3	2	1

Featured Interval in exercises 16-18: Major 6th

examples:

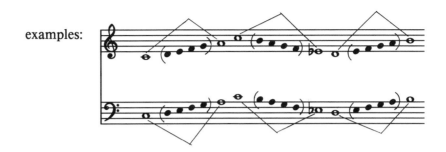

16. Key: F major

do sol mi sol mi re do mi sol do
1 5 3 5 3 2 1 3 5 1

17. Key: Eb major

do mi sol la do la ti do
1 3 5 6 1 6 7 1

18. Key: D minor

la ti do la do do ti la ti do la
1 2 3 1 3 3 2 1 2 3 1

Featured Interval in exercises 19-21: minor 6th

examples:

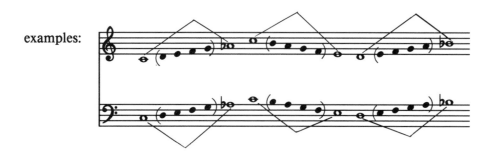

19. Key: C minor

20. Key: C major

21. Key: D minor

Featured Interval in exercises 22-24: Major 7th

examples:

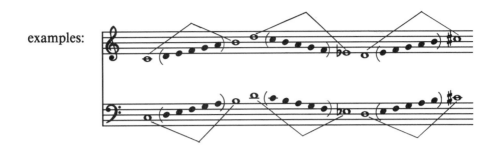

22. Key: C major

do re mi fa sol la ti do
1 2 3 4 5   6 7 1

do mi sol do do ti la do ti la sol
1   3   5   1   1   7   6   1   7   6   5

23. Key: C minor

 (harmonic minor scale)

la ti do re mi fa si la
1 2 3 4 5 6 7# 1

la ti do re mi fa si la la si la
1   2 3   4   5   6   7   1   1   7   1

24. Key: D major

do re mi fa sol la ti do
1 2 3 4 5   6 7 1

do ti do la do ti do sol do ti do fa mi re do
1 7 1   6   1 7 1   5   1 7 1   4   3   2   1

78

Featured Interval in exercises 25-27: minor 7th

examples:

25. Key: F major

do re mi fa sol la ti do
1 2 3 4 5   6 7 1

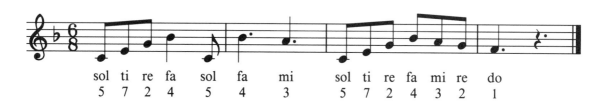

sol ti re fa sol fa mi   sol ti re fa mi re do
5   7 2 4 5   4 3   5   7 2 4 3 2 1

26. Key: D minor

la ti do re mi fa sol la
1 2 3 4 5 6 7   1

la do mi sol la sol fa mi   la do mi sol la   la
1 3 5 7   1 7   6 5   1 3 5 7   1   1

27. Key: G major

la do mi fa sol la ti do
1 2 3 4 5   6 7 1

sol fa mi sol sol fa mi   sol fa mi sol do   do
5   4 3 5   5   4 3   5   4 3 5   1   1

Featured Interval in exercises 28-30: minor 2nd (half step)

examples:

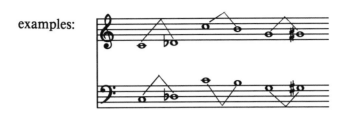

28. Key: C minor

29. Key: Bb major

30. Key: C major

Featured Interval in exercises 31-33: Octave

examples:

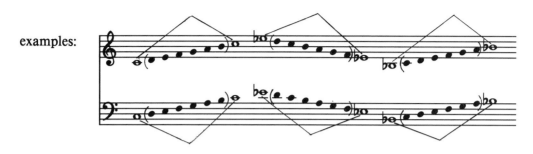

31. Key: D♭ major

do re mi fa sol la ti do
1 2 3 4 5   6 7 1

do   do   do mi sol do   sol   do   do   do
1   1   1 3 5   1   5   1   1   1

32. Key: C minor

la ti do re mi fa sol la
1 2 3 4 5 6 7   1

mi la la la la do mi   mi la la la la
5 1 1 1 1 3 5   5 1 1 1 1

33. Key: D major

do re mi fa sol la ti do
1 2 3 4 5   6 7 1

do do   do   do do mi sol do do do do   do
1 1   1   1 1 3   5   1 1 1 1   1

Featured Interval in exercises 34-36: Tritone
This interval can also be called an Augmented 4th (a 4th extended by a half step) or a Diminished 5th (a 5th lessened by a half step)

Further Exercises

1. Key: B minor

la ti do re mi fa sol la
1   2   3   4   5   6   7   1

la
1

2. Key: E♭ Major

do re mi fa sol la ti do
1   2   3   4   5   6   7   1

do
1

3. Key: D minor

la ti do re mi fi si la
1   2   3   4   5   6♯ 7♯ 1

la
1

4. Key C Major

5. Key: G Major

6. Key: D major

7. Key: F major

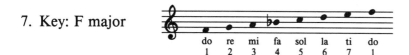

do re mi fa sol la ti do
1 2 3 4 5   6 7 1

do
1

8. Key: A Major

do re mi fa sol la ti do
1 2 3 4 5   6 7 1

sol
5

9. Key: E Major

do re mi fa sol la ti do
1 2 3 4 5   6 7 1

do
1

10. Key: F Major

sol
5

11. Key: C Major

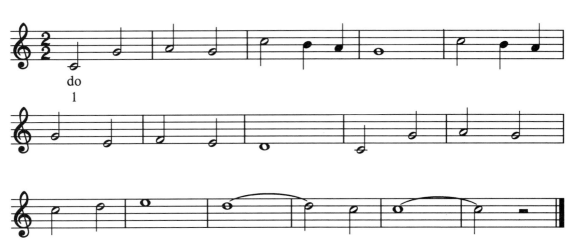

do
1

86

12. Key: E minor

la ti do re mi fa sol la
1   2   3   4   5   6   7   1

la
1

13. Key: F Major

do re mi fa sol la ti do
1   2   3   4   5   6   7   1

sol
5

14. Key: F Major

15. Key: G Major

16. Key: C Major

do re mi fa sol la ti do
1   2   3   4   5   6   7   1

mi
3

17. Key: E♭ Major

do re mi fa sol la ti do
1   2   3   4   5   6   7   1

do
1

18. Key: B♭ Major

do re mi fa sol la ti do
1   2   3   4   5   6   7   1

mi
3

19. Key: D Major

20. Key: E♭ Major

Rounds for Sight Singing

1.

Hey! Ho! to the green-wood go—— And there find buck and doe.

2.

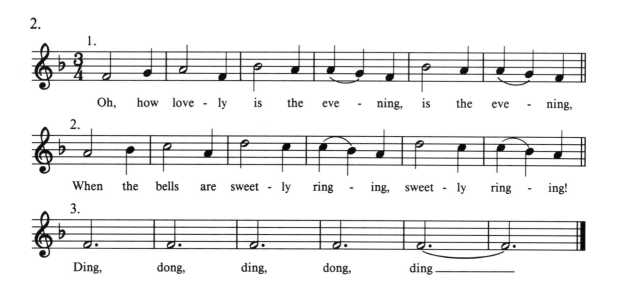

Oh, how love - ly is the eve - ning, is the eve - ning,

When the bells are sweet - ly ring - ing, sweet - ly ring - ing!

Ding, dong, ding, dong, ding————

3.

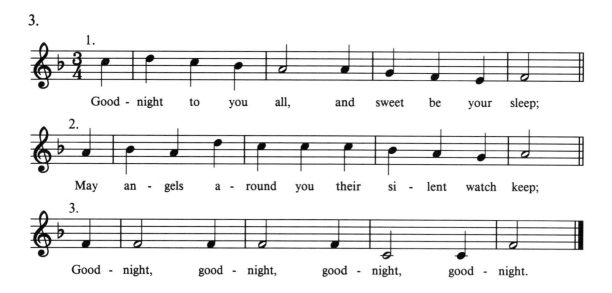

Good - night to you all, and sweet be your sleep;

May an - gels a - round you their si - lent watch keep;

Good - night, good - night, good - night, good - night.

4.

Who'll buy my po - sies fresh, Lil - lies and ros - es, With

cow - slips and prim - ros - es, La - dies, who'll buy?

5.

Come, fol - low, fol - low, fol - low, fol - low, fol - low,

fol - low me! Whith-er shall I fol - low, fol - low, fol - low,

Whith - er shall I fol - low, fol - low thee?

To the green - wood, to the green - wood,

To the green - wood, green - wood tree.

Practicing Thirds in 2 parts

Verse

There's a low green valley by the old Ken-tuck-y

shore, Where we've whiled man-y hap-py hours a-way,

A - sit-ting and a-sing-ing by the lit-tle cot-tage

door, Where lived my dar-ling Nel-lie Gray.

Chorus

Oh, my poor Nel-lie Gray, they have tak-en you a-

way, And I'll nev-er see my dar-ling an-y-more.

I'm a-sit-ting by the riv-er and I'm weep-ing all the

day, For you've gone from the old Ken-tuck-y shore.

Three Part Treble Reading

The cruel war is rag - ing,
To - mor - row is Sun - day,

John - ny has to fight, I want to be
Mon - day is the day your cap - tain calls

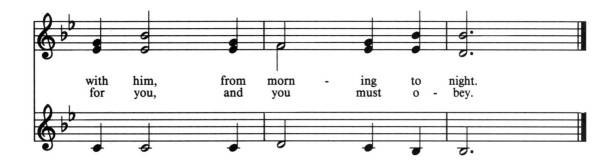

with him, from morn - ing to night.
for you, and you must o - bey.

94

Reading Material for 2 part boys voices

Four Part Reading

1.

My coun - try, 'tis of thee, sweet land of
My na - tive coun - try, thee, land of the
Let mu - sic swell the breeze, and ring from
Our fa - thers' God, to thee, au - thor of

lib - er - ty, of thee I sing; land where my
no - ble free, thy name I love; I love thy
all the trees sweet free - dom's song; let mor - tal
lib - er - ty, to thee we sing; long may our

fa - thers died, land of the pil - grim's pride,
rocks and rills, thy woods and tem - pled hills;
tongues a - wake, let all that breathe par - take,
land be bright with free - dom's ho - ly light;

from ev - ery moun - tain - side let free - dom ring.
my heart with rap - ture thrills like that a - bove.
let rocks their si - lence break, the sound pro - long.
pro - tect us by thy might, great God, our King.

96

Ludwig van Beethoven
from the Ninth Symphony

2.

Joy, thou spark from flame im - mor - tal, Daugh - ter of E - ly - si - um!

Drunk with fire o heav'n born god - dess, We in - vade thy hal - i - dom!

Let thy mag - ic bring to - geth - er All whom earth born lands di - vide; All___

___ man - kind shall be as broth - ers, 'Neath thy ten - der wings and wide.

3.

Franz Joseph Haydn

O blest Cre - a - tor, source of light, you
You joined the morn and eve - ning ray; you

gave the day with splen - dor bright, when
found it good and called it "day." But

on the new and liv - ing earth you
now the threat - ening dark - ness nears— we

brought all things to glo - rious birth.
pray you, Fa - ther, calm our fears.

98

Thy Truth, which never varies

4.

Martin Luther
English version by
John Haberkorn

J.S. Bach

Thy Truth, which nev - er va - ries, Thy Love, that

nev - er wea - ries, Grant us and all that

say then Through Christ a faith - ful A - men.

A BRIEF HISTORY OF CHORAL MUSIC

Has there always been music?

What songs did children of 100,000 years ago sing? Unfortunately, we don't know. While researchers can piece together speculations about human culture of thousands, even perhaps millions of years ago, we know virtually nothing about music as it existed on this world before the times of the ancient Greeks and Romans. The music of long ago was never written down nor recorded by any means, so it remains forever a mystery. Even with no evidence we can probably safely assume two things: (1) Music of some kind certainly existed even in the earliest days of human history, and (2) this earliest music was undoubtedly played on the oldest instrument of this world, the human voice. Singing has always been, and remains to be, the universal musical expression simply because everyone has a voice!

ANCIENT GREEK CIVILIZATION

Major Historical Events

B.C. 800-461	City states in Greece are established and flourish
776	First Olympic Games
753	Traditional date that Rome was founded
387	Plato founds the Academy
336-323	Alexander the Great conquers the known world
146	Roman invaders conquer Greece
49	Julius Caesar becomes Emperor of Rome

Music

Greek philosophers, such as Pythagoras, write about the mathematical relationships in music. Modern music theory begins.

Visual Arts

The Golden Age in Greece (480-404) produces great works of architecture (such as the Parthenon) and sculpture (*Discuss Thrower* by Myron). Later Greek art, dating from the first and second centuries B.C., is of the Hellenistic period (*Venus de Milo* and *Winged Victory of Samothrace*).

Literature

Greek dramatists: Sophocles, Euripides, Aristophones
Greek philosophers: Socrates, Plato, Aristotle, Aesop
Greek poets: Homer, Heslod, Sappho

Historians have very little firsthand knowledge of early music of the ancient world, first because it was not written down and second, because most of it was freely improvised. Art of the period and treatises on music give evidence of the importance of music in the life of early Greece. Music played a vital role in Grecian drama, brought grandeur to governmental ceremonies, heightened the passion of Greek poetry, called men to battle, and most important, was crucial to the religious ritual. Early greek music probably consisted of a single line of melody sung in octaves and sometimes accompanied by stringed instruments. The Greek philosophers also gave us the first known theories of music, and their writings tell us their ideas of how music should be constructed and what it means in ideal terms.

THE EARLY CHRISTIAN ERA

Major Historical Events

A.D. 65	Christians first persecuted in Rome
284	Era of the late Roman Empire begins; Diocletian rules Rome.
395	Separation of Eastern and Western Roman Empires
410	Rome invaded by Germanic tribes; Saxons and Angles invade Britain
476	Traditional date marking the end of the Roman Empire
ca.650	Monasteries are established and flourish (later becoming the center of musical life)
800	Charlemagne crowned Emperor by the Pope
871	Alfred the Great becomes King of England

Music

ca.600	Pope Gregory organizes the chants of the church for use in the Roman Catholic liturgy, thus this music was called Gregorian Chant
800-900	Music is cultivated in the monasteries

Visual Arts

70	Colosseum begun at Rome
118-126	Pantheon constructed
	Two distinct styles of art arose in Europe: the Byzantine style, the influence of Constantinople (churches at Ravenna, Italy) and the Islamic style, the early Moslem influence (mosque at Cordoba, Spain)

Literature

Roman poets: Vergil, Horace, Ovid
New Testament is written
Christian Writers: Ambrose, Jerome, Augustine

Although we have little knowledge of music of the Roman empire, we can assume that it was generally borrowed from the Greek culture. As the early Christian church became more and more of an influence, so then did the major thrust in European Music drastically change. As long as the Greek style of Music was predominant the music was secular (or non-religious). Much of the music of the Greeks and Romans was probably ceremonial music, played at certain public occasions, or as part of a drama. The musical life in Europe continued to be centered around ceremonies and special occasions, but of a vastly different nature. The church service and the life of the church clearly became the focus of virtually all musical activity from the third century on, dominating music over the next thousand years.

Music of The Early Church

Offering praise to God through singing was a vital part of the Hebrew culture. The Old Testament gives numerous accounts of organized singing in ancient Israel. The Book of Chronicles accounts for a systematic musical culture, centered in the Temple and organized by the Levites who were appointed to supply 4,000 musicians for the religious services. A choir school was organized and maintained to train the cantors (soloists) and the choristers (singers in the choir) for the Temple. Early choral performances in the Temple consisted of antiphonal (alternating choirs) and responsorial singing (alternation of choir and soloist). The congregations of the Temple rarely participated in the service but would occasionally respond with short verbal statements such as "amen" or "hallelujah." The music of the early church was prepared and performed by professional singers who were paid and who were furnished homes.

The early Christian Church followed the practices of the Jewish Temple in that the singing was responsorial or antiphonal. When Christianity was recognized as an official religion in 313, St. Sylvester, who was Pope from 314 to 336, founded the first singing school or schola cantorum. The school was dedicated to the instruction and training of singers for the papal choir. Eventually the monasteries became dedicated to the training of basic musical skills and served as the centers of early choral music education.

Gregorian Chant

The first musical center for Christian music was in Milan, where Bishop Ambrose was the first to write down a uniform collection of songs and texts (Ambrosian chants) for Church use. Two centuries later, Pope Gregory I (reigned 590-604) undertook a similar task of greater importance and proportion. He reformed the liturgy of the Church and established a uniform repertoire of 3,000 chants for specific use by the Roman Catholic Church. The chants (which came to be known as Gregorian Chants) follow the calendar of the Roman Catholic Church and are especially important because they are the musical inspiration for the later development of important musical forms, particularly the mass and motet.

Chants consist solely of single line melodies sung in unison. There are no harmonies or chords played or sung along with these chant melodies . Choirs at this time were made up exclusively of male singers who almost always sang a cappella (or unaccompanied by instruments). Women only sang in the convent choirs, and never in public. Plainsong is another term that is used in referring to chants of this period. The notated plainsong melodies that survive from that time only show the notes of the tune, giving little indication of the rhythm. It is generally believed that these chants were sung in a free flowing style without a steady beat. Choirs at this time did not have the kind of directors which we have today, but probably simply had a leader who guided the group through his singing, not through actual conducting.

MEDIEVAL EUROPE

MEDIEVAL EUROPE

Major Historical Events

ca.900-1200	Feudalism dominates as the basic system for society
ca.1000	The Vikings reach North America
1066	Norman conquest of Britain
1000-1300	Age of Chivalry & Knights flourish
1096	First crusade
1167	Oxford University Founded
1209	St. Francis of Assisi founds the Franciscan Order
1215	Magna Carta signed by King John of England
1275-1292	Marco Polo introduces Asian culture to Europe
1348	The Black Death runs rampant
1431	Joan of Arc burned at the Stake
1453	The Hundred Years War Ends

Music

ca.900	Two and three part music begins to appear (called organum)
1025	Guido of Arezzo, the father of modern music notation, makes his first writings on the subject
1073	Winchester Tropes collected. A trope was an addition at appropriate points to a chant melody. Originally, these were simply vocal improvisations but later became traditional. Texts were also added to these flights of chant melody.
1150	Troubadours flourish in France, and with them the growth of secular song.
1175	The Cathedral of Notre Dame in Paris emerges as the musical center of Europe, led by two composers, Leonin and Perotin.
1200	Trouveres become popular in France, Minnesingers in Germany, and with them the further growth of secular song.
1240	The motet becomes the dominant type of sacred music.
1360	Guillaume Machaut's Messe de Notre Dame
1400	The Burgundian School (or style) of music begins to emerge, its principal composers being Guillaume Dufay and Gilles Binchois

Visual Arts

1000	Romanesque style of architecture emerges
1094	St. Marks Cathedral begun in Venice
1150	Gothic Style of architecture begins
1163	Notre Dame begun in Paris
1305	Giotto paints chapel frescoes in Italy
1308	Siena panels begun by Italian painter Duccio

Literature

Italian Poets:	Petrarch, Dante (*The Divine Comedy*, 1307), Boccaccio (December, 1353)

Music in Medieval Europe took a dramatic turn around the year 900 with the introduction of polyphony, or music of two or more parts. Originally, this early polyphony was a simple harmonization of the chant at a fourth, fifth or octave below the melody. This style of music is called organum. As the centuries passed, the harmonizing part or parts became much freer and eventually evolved into independent counter melodies to the main tune. Another important development of this period was the use of instruments to accompany choirs. For many centuries music had strictly been vocal music, but gradually the use of church organs, strings and wind instruments became more acceptable. Even so, choirs still dominated musical life, the instruments used only as an accompaniment.

Although church music, or sacred music, still was the main current of activity, non-religious music began to play a minor role in Europe. The first style of secular song was sung by troubadours in the south of France. These were singers and storytellers who travelled all over the continent, entertaining people in the towns and countryside as they passed through. In northern France these performers were called trouveres. In Germany, travelling poet-musicians were called minnesingers. These secular songs were different from the church music in several ways. Most notably, they were in the everyday language of the people. All church music continued to be in Latin at this time. The style of music was also much lighter than church music, more like folk music.

But the music of the church continued to lead the way. The cathedral of Notre Dame in Paris emerged as the musical center of Europe around the year 1175, and remained the most important source of music for several centuries. Almost all music prior to this time is anonymous—we simply don't know who composed it. At Notre Dame some individually known composers became an important part of music history. Three important composers associated with this Parisian center are Leonin, Perotin and Guillaume Machaut.

There are two significant types of polyphonic compositions which emerge in sacred music of this period. A motet is a piece written for unaccompanied choir based on a sacred Latin text. These short pieces were written to be inserted into the regular church mass, although they are not a part of the liturgy. In a general way one could think of these motets as the "choir anthem" part of a church service. Motets began being composed around 1240, and although musical styles changed, motets were still being written and performed by choirs 500 years later. The other important development was the trend of having an entire mass (which was always sung) written by one composer. Up until this time the different movements of mass (the liturgy) were simply collections of anonymous compositons. Guillaume Machaut is the first known musician to compose music for an entire mass, to be performed from start to finish as a church service. His first composition of this type is the famous "Messe de Notre Dame", written in 1360.

Guillaume Machaut (ca. 1300-1377), was an important French composer, widely believed to be the first great composer of European music. As a young man he studied theology and took holy orders. For 17 years he was notary and secretary to King John of Bohemia, a position which allowed him to travel extensively over the continent. At 40 he moved to Rheims, France where he lived until his death. Professionally he was always a clergyman, although he must have spent a good deal of time composing music. Machaut was a versatile musician and wrote a wide variety of pieces during his lifetime. His "Messe de Notre Dame", although seldom heard in modern times, secures for him a lasting place of honor in history, for it is surely the most important piece of music from the entire era.

To conclude, the "Gothic" period of history is important in the development of music in a few key ways. A system of standard musical notation emerged and stabilized during this period which not only allowed clear indication of pitches, but also of rhythm. This in itself invited musicians to compose music in specific, detailed ways that had not been possible up until this time. It also allowed rather complex works to become relatively well-known, since competent musicians could learn music simply from working with a copy of a manuscript. In all of music history up until this time music had been passed on in an oral tradition to a great degree.

It was a time of a great deal of progress in technical ways, but also was a time of relative stability of aesthetics. "Aesthetics" is the general purpose and point of view that any creator has in making a work of art. The Gothic aesthetic was to glorify God, but not in a personal, passionate way. At this time in history the attitude toward God (which really defined the entire culture) was one of awe and humility. The arts during this time are not personal, since that would call attention to the artist, but formal and strictly comply to certain rules which had become accepted. The music of the 14th century composer's detached, cerebral execution of the formal style was far more important than any subjective self-expression, and might be described as learned, academic and complex.

The last important musical trend of the middle ages is the rise of the Burgundian style in the first half of the 15th century, a label that is applied to music during the reign of Philip The Good, Duke of Burgundy (Belgium), a great patron of the arts. This style of music was found throughout central Europe at the time, and did not emininate from any single city. The general thrust of this style was a reaction against the strictly formal style of the preceding century. Burgundian composers strove for a sweeter, less austere musical language, in many ways much simpler than the complex and comparatively dry, dense, academic style of the 14th century. A very important development was the heightened use of various instrumental combinations. Dissimilar instruments, such as recorders, viols (stringed instruments) and trombones combined for the first time, and the instrumental ensemble became an important musical presence.

Guillaume Dufay (1400-1474) was the leading composer of the Burgundian school. He received a thorough music training at an early age as a choir boy at the Cathedral of Cambrai, later becoming chapel master (director of music) at this same cathedral. In 1428 he moved to Rome where he was a member of the Papal chapel musical staff. After a few other moves, in which he was in the service of the Duke of Savoy, he settled in Cambrai, his hometown, in 1445, where he was the most esteemed and honored musician of the entire region. He lived a very comfortable life there until his death in 1474. Dufay wrote a great deal of music in his lifetime, mastering every sacred and secular form and style of his day. Not only did he excel in writing masses, motets and other church music, he was a gifted composer of the chanson (secular French choral music of the time).

Gilles Binchois (1400-1460) was born into a family of honored position in a court in France at Hainout. He quickly advanced as a church musician to a position of high responsibility in the Burgundian Court, but curiously is best remembered for his secular compositions. Binchois is perhaps the first major composer in music history to write primarily non-religious music. Up until the first half of the 15th century, writing music meant writing church music almost exclusively, with very few exceptions.

The dramatic changes brought about by the Burgundian school of composers are good clues to the next great age of history that was soon to appear in its full glory, the Renaissance.

THE RENAISSANCE

Although there is some disagreement among historians as to when the Renaissance actually began, the most common definition of this period in music is 1450-1600.

Major Historical Events

1434	The Medici family comes to power in Italy, and remains an important supporter of the arts throughout the rest of the century.
1450	Humanism emerges in Italy
1454	Gutenberg invents the printing press
1492	Columbus discovers North America
1513	Balboa discovers the Pacific ocean
1517	Martin Luther begins the Protestant Reformation
1519-1522	Magellan makes the first voyage around the world
1558	Queen Elizabeth begins reign over England
1563	The Church of England is established
1582	Pope Gregory XIII makes a major calendar reform
1588	British defeat of the Spanish Armada

Music

1450	The Flemish School begins to emerge, defining the new spirit of the music of the Renaissance. The most important composers, spanning a hundred years, in this group are: Johannes Ockeghem, Jacob Obrecht, Henrik Isaac, Josquin des Pres, Adriaen Willaert, Jacob Arcadelt, Orlando di Lasso.
1498	The first license to print music was granted to Ottaviano de Petrucci of Venice; birth of music publishing.
1525	Birth of Giovanni Pierluigi da Palestrina, the leading composer of the Roman School and the greatest composer of sacred music of the Renaissance.
1525	The "Golden Age" of English music begins, the most important composers being Thomas Tallis, Orlando Gibbons, William Byrd, John Wilbye, Thomas Morley
1533	The first full fledged Italian madrigals appear.
ca.1550	Mature instrumental forms emerge.
ca.1550	Protestant music emerges as a style separate from Catholic music.
1554	Birth of Giovanni Gabrielli, leading composer of the Venetian School.
1567	Birth of Claudio Monteverdi, one of the greatest of Italian Madrigalists and an important transitional composer into the Baroque.

Visual Arts

Leading artists of the early Italian Renaissance: Fra Angelico, Botticelli, Donatello
Leading artists of the early Northern Renaissance: Van Eyck, Durer, Grunewald

Leading artists of the later Renaissance: Leonardo da Vinci, Raphael, Michelangelo, Titian

Literature

Important French Writers: Villon, Racine, Moliere, Descartes
Important British Writers: Edmund Spenser, John Donne, Ben Johnson, William Shakespeare
Although some of these writers continued to work after 1600, their works are still classified as belonging to the Renaissance.

Humanism

The term "Renaissance," like "Gothic" for the late Middle Ages and "Baroque" for the 150 years following the Renaissance, was borrowed from art history. Its literal meaning, "rebirth," appropriately categorizes the artists, sculptors, and architects who looked to the past achievements of the ancient world of Greece and Rome to create masterpieces in their own time. The term is somewhat misleading in that it implies a sudden rebirth and awakening of the arts and of learning in a world covered by the ignorance and cultural void of the Middle Ages. History moves slowly and, upon reflection, it can be loosely organized into certain groupings of time according to pattern changes in daily life, culture, history, and science.

The Renaissance marks a significant change from a sacred-oriented society to a society that was secularly oriented; a society in which man, not God, was the central figure. The rebirth was an awakening of the human spirit. "Humanism," as it was called, stressed the virtues of the living man. The Renaissance writers and poets spread the ideal that man had rights, inner strengths, and worthy personal feelings. Humanist writers began to use secular subject matter so that their works might be acceptable not only to God through their religious writings, but also to living men through their secular writings.

The high Renaissance produced such great artists as da Vinci, Michelangelo, Titian, Durer, and Holbein. Literature matched artistic greatness with Machiavelli in Italy, Rabelais, Montaigne, and Ronsard in France, Cervantes in Spain, and Shakespeare, Spencer, Bacon, and Ben Johnson in England. The field of science felt the awakening spirit in Copernicus and Galileo. Explorers such as Columbus were eager to discover the world around them. Religion also underwent a major change in the form of the Protestant Reformation, led by Martin Luther.

Music Printing

The rise of music printing was especially important to the development of music. The practice of printing books from movable type, as perfected by Johann Gutenberg in 1450, was applied to music printing. The first collection of music printed from movable type was published in 1501 by Ottaviano de' Petrucci in Venice.

Function of Music

Music played a very important part of life in the Renaissance. The well-educated man was expected to be an amateur musician who could read music and perform as an instrumentalist or as a singer. Every monarch in Europe was interested in music and many of them were good players or singers. The art of the period testifies to the fact that music literacy was not restricted to the artistocracy but was an important part of daily life. Many paintings illustrate the peasant or lowly shepherd with lute in hand enjoying music by singing. The Renaissance was a period of intense growth in the field of music, especially vocal music.

The Flemish School

The Flemish school is so named because many of the important composers came from the southern part of Belgium (Flanders). However, it was not a national style, but an international movement of great significance. The most important overall characteristic of these composers is that they created a new polyphonic style in which all the parts of a composition (i.e., soprano, alto, tenor, bass) are balanced to be equally important. The musical device most commonly employed to achieve this balance is what is called imitation. This is achieved by having a musical motive (or group of notes) repeated and exchanged by different voices in the texture. Masses and motets are the predominant genres (types of pieces) by these Flemish composers, although several characteristic secular styles emerged and flourished. While instrumental compositions began to become increasingly important, it was style music for the choir, most often a cappella, that ruled the day.

An example of this style from the choral repertory collections in **Something New to Sing About** is "O Bella Fusa" by Orlando di Lasso.

The Roman School

This type of sacred music written for the Catholic Church was established by its leading composer, Giovanni Pierluigi di Palestrina. It is a style of music written exclusively for the a cappella choir. Palestrina established the most influential style of Renaissance counterpoint. Counterpoint is a term meaning the relationship of two or more moving musical lines. Palestrina's style of counterpoint, so clearly refined in its voice leading, was so important that even today musicians still study it to learn techniques of composition. In contrapuntal styles of music (music based on the full use of counterpoint) only J. S. Bach rivals Palestrina as the greatest composer of this type of music.

One of Palestrina's many followers in Rome was Francesco Suriano, and his "Regina Caeli" appears in the Something New to Sing About choral collection.

The Italian Madrigal

Of all the secular musical forms which emerged during the Renaissance, the most important is the madrigal. These are always compositions for an unaccompanied choir. The true madrigal did not appear until 1533, although it developed from earlier, similar types of pieces. The poetry on which madrigals are based are most often about romantic love, and can be either simple flirtations, earnest, or tragically heart-breaking. A common occurence in madrigals is word painting, a device a composer uses to specifically express certain key words in a poem. For instance, on the word "fly" a composer may write a quickly ascending melody to create the impression of flight.

There were many composers of the Italian madrigal, some of whom are from The Flemish School of composers. A highlighted list of great Italian madrigalists includes: Orlando di Lasso, Luca Marenzio, Gesualdo and Claudio Monteverdi. Even today there are many choral ensembles who specialize in the works of these and other madrigal composers.

The English Madrigalists

The British composers of the 16th and early 17th centuries rivalled the Italians in developing their own Madrigal style. While the English madrigal composers initially wrote in the Italian style, they eventually developed a clearly different style from their neighbors to the south. The difference between the English and Italian language brought about some of these English adaptations. Madrigals are written in intimate association to the words of a poem, and naturally the flow and feel of the English language is very much different from that of the Italian language. Beyond this, the English madrigals tend to exhibit more pure merriment than the Italian variety.

The Venetian School

The great cathedral of St. Mark's in Venice became important as the center for an important group of composers of the Renaissance known as the Venetian School. Their unique style of composition was directly related to the architecture of the cathedral. Built in the eleventh century, the plan of the church is a Greek cross of equal arms, covered by a large central dome and by a dome over each of the arms of the cross. The domes of the church (facing each other) served as choir lofts, each with its own organ. The architectural plan, with its spacious interior, rounded domes, and gold mosaics, inispired the composers who served as maestro di cappella (Choirmaster). The cathedral was the chapel of the Doge, the ruler of the small independent city state of Venice.

The music of the composers of the Venetian School has three important characteristics which are directly influenced by either the architecture of the cathedral or by the splendor of the city of Venice:

1. Music that is written for two or more choirs (polychoral) who sing alternately or together in a blend of chordal and imitative musical textures.

2. Rich textures of choral sound (men's voices and women's voices used in alternation or mixed voices in alternating choirs) and contrasting textures of voices and instruments.

3. Boldness of harmonies.

The greatest of the Venetian composers was Giovanni Gabrieli (1557-1612), nephew of Andrea Gabrieli (ca. 1510-1586). Giovanni Gabrieli's music expanded the Venetian style to include up to five choirs (one for each of the domes in St. Mark's), each with different combinations of high and low voices and each combined with instruments of different timbres. Gabrieli's music marks the first use of the words piano and forte which he used to indicate solo (piano) or tutti (forte) statements.

The Venetian School was admired as the most progressive in all of Italy, and it was an important influence on other composers of the Renaissance. Pupils of the Gabrielis came to Venice to study and carried the influence of their teachers to their native countries: Germany was represented by Heinrich Schütz (1585-1672), Hieronymus Praetorius (1560-1629), and Hans Leo Hassler (1524-1612), Czechoslovakia by Jacob Handl or Jacobus Gallus (1550-1591), and Italy by Claudio Monterverdi (1567-1643).

The Protestant Reformation

Perhaps the most dramatic event in the history of Christian religion was the Protestant Reformation of the sixteenth century. The Reformation was a revolt against many of the long-standing practices of the Roman Catholic Church. Because it was a religious revolt, it affected the music of the church and had a strong influence on the development of musical style. Led by Martin Luther (1483-1546), the conflict was centered in Germany but it spread quickly to other countries, especially France and England. Luther had strong feelings about the importance of music in the church. His main concern was that the music did not directly involve the congregation and that the continued use of Latin as the church language could not speak directly to the people. His reforms included many important principles: first, he substituted the traditional Latin words of the church ritual with German words; second, he encouraged congregational participation in the worship service through responsive readings and prayers; and third, he introduced hymn singing in the church. Until this time, all of the music in the church had been prepared by professional musicians. The Chorale or Kirchenlied (church song), as it was called, was a hymn with German words set to a melody in verse fashion and sung by the entire congregation. The chorale became the backbone of the Lutheran worship service and inspired great composers such as Heinrich Schütz and Johann Sebastian Bach (1685-

1750) to elaborate on its content and to expand its form to create new musical forms, the cantata and the Passion.

Renaissance Style

From one point of view, the history of musical style could be seen as a constant battle between certain basic principles of musical compositon: emphasis on the harmony of the music or emphasis on the melody of the music (homophony versus polyphony). The Renaissance period is identified as a period of intense growth in the melodic aspect of musical composition. Music of this period is primarily linear; that is, each part (for voices or instruments) is equally important, melodically independent, and serves to reinforce the important melodies in the composition through imitation.

The Renaissance was a time in which a cappella music flourished. The term a cappella literally means "for the chapel." Although a cappella music was originally written for the church, today the term is interpreted as music which is performed by voices alone and is not restricted to sacred music only. The sixteenth century has come to be known as "the Golden Age of A cappella music."

The music of the Renaissance was written in imitative style; that is, one voice part sings a vocal line which is then imitated by each of the other voice parts. The greatest composer of the imitative style was Giovanni Pierluigi da Palestrina (ca. 1525-1594) who was maestro di cappella at St. Peter's Cathedral in Rome. His music was the perfect example of order, restraint, balance, and good taste. Other composers imitated his style of composition and his music stood as the ideal model for other composers.

Because the emphasis in Renaissance music is on melody, the music has no strict rhythmic phrasing. It was not metered (there was no time signature and no barlines) and therefore the patterns of regular groupings of strong and weak beats did not exist. Renaissance music was governed by the musical organization of the melodic line giving it a linear emphasis and weakening the groupings of beats.

Renaissance music is not bound to traditional rules of harmony. The harmony results from the sounding of the melodic lines in combination and is not ruled by order or function.

Renaissance vocal music is closely bound to the words; that is, the words determine the tempo, mood, dynamics, and musical phrasing of the composition. Renaissance composers did not use dynamic markings or tempo indications; first, because they usually prepared the performances of their own music and therefore could tell performers how they wanted their own music to be sung or played; second, because tempo and dynamic markings had not yet been invented; and third, because performance practices were generally understood by the performers.

The Renaissance is represented in Something New to Sing About by these additional pieces: (1) "Chi la Gagliarda" by Donato, (2) "Sing We and Chant It" by Morley, (3) "Lo, How a Rose E'er Blooming" by Praetorious (presented in SATB and SSA settings).

Important Renaissance Composers

William Byrd (c. 1543-1623) was an Elizabethan composer and one of the most important English musicians of all time. Very little is know of his early life, but he was appointed organist of the Lincoln Cathedral on Feb. 27, 1563 and a gentleman of the Chapel Royal (i.e. a singer) in London on Feb. 22, 1570. He continued to hold both posts until Dec. of 1572 when he left the Lincoln Cathedral and settled in London. He published several works with Thomas Tallis, another composer of the time, and his association with Tallis appears on the issue, in 1575, of a license giving the two of them a monopoly on printing and publishing music. When Tallis died in 1585, the license passed on to Byrd as the surviving partner.

In 1568, Byrd married Juliana Birley and by 1577 had four or five children. It was in this year that Byrd and Tallis petitioned the Queen for financial help with the license of printing and publishing music. It is interesting to note that Byrd was a Roman Catholic holding several appointments in the Anglican church and was constantly at odds with the officials of the church and government in London because of this. There were, however, never any serious threats or attempts to replace him in any of these posts. In fact, when he died in 1623, he was described in the records of the Royal Chapel as a "Father of Music."

He published numerous sacred works for both the Catholic church and the Anglican church during his lifetime. He also published many works for the keyboard, including the virginal, which was a popular keyboard instrument in Elizabethan times. Byrd was not strictly a Madrigalist, and in general his temperament seems to have inclined him more towards church music than secular composition. The highest point of his creative ability is to be found in his three masses and the Latin motets where, on his own admission, the texts provided him with inspiration. He died on July 4, 1623 and a complete edition of his works has been published by Edmund H. Fellows in volumes (1937-1950).

Josquin Des Prez (c. 1440-1521) was born in the province of Hainaut which is in the present Franco-Belgian border region. From 1473 to at least 1479 he was a choirmember of the Ducal Chapel of the Sforza family in Milan and remained under the patronage of the Cardinal Sforza until Sforza's death in 1505. There is also reference to Des Prez from time to time in the Papal Chapel in Rome, and in France during the reign of Louis the XII. In 1503 Des Prez was appointed the Maestro di Capella at the court of Ferrara, but in the year he left for France. In the latter half of his life he returned to his Natal region (Hainaut) and died at Conde Sur-L'Escaut in 1521. He was known throughout Europe and was called "the Father of Musicians", and "Master of Notes" and the "Best Composer of our time" by many of his contemporaries. Few musicians have enjoyed higher renown while they lived, or exercised more profound and lasting influence on those who came up after him. Out of an extraordinary number of composers who lived around 1500 he must be counted among the greatest of all time.

His compositions were published in large numbers of 16th century printed collections, and also occur in many of the manuscripts of the time. He wrote, altogether, about 18 masses, 100 motets, and 70 chansons as well as other secular vocal works. Very few of his works can be dated accurately, but it is apparent that his music contains traditional and modern elements. He is the composer who, more than any other, may be said to stand at the border between the middle ages and the modern world. The conservative elements of his music are most conspicuous in the masses, while the more modern aspects occur in his secular works. Josquin was particularly praised by his contemporaries for the care he took to suit his music to the text. In addition, it may be said that his music shows the increasing pull of Dominant - Tonic, foreshadowing later tonal practices.

Josquin was a composer of the period of transition between Medieval and modern times, much like Monteverdi was a bridge between Renaissance and Baroque; Handel between Baroque and Classical and Beethoven between Classical and Romantic eras. Josquin and Beethoven resemble each other in many other ways. In both, the strong impulse of personal utterance struggled against the limits of the musical language of their time. Both worked slowly and deliberately on their music making numerous revisions along the way to the finished product. Both had a sense of humor. Both, because of their independent attitudes, had trouble with their patrons. Both, in their best works, achieved a combination of intensity and order, individuality and universality, which is a mark of true genious.

Orlando di Lasso (c.1532-1594) Born in Mons, Belgium, di Lasso was trained as a choirboy in the service of the church. His voice was so beautiful that he was kidnapped three times in vain attempts to secure him as a singer in various churches. Di Lasso's singing career took him first to Sicily in the service of Ferdinando Gonzaga, viceroy of Sicily. When Gonzaga was transferred, di Lasso went with him, first to Palermo and then to Milan. Eventually he was appointed to the court of Albert V of Bavaria in Munich. He is known by several names: Roland de Lassus (Belgian), Orlando di Lasso (Italian), Orlandus Lassus (Latin), and Rolande de Lattre (French). He was knighted by both Emperor Maximilian II and the Pope.

One of the most prolific and versatile of all Renaissance vocal composers, di Lasso was called the "Belgian Orpheus" and the "Prince of Music." His importance as a composer lies in the fact that his music embraces the flavor and style of several countries. He was a master composer of Italian madrigals, German lieder, French chansons, and Latin motets. He wrote over 2,000 works (all vocal), representing every style of vocal music of his time: 53 masses, 500 motets, 133 French chansons, 100 magnificats, numerous Italian madrigals, German Lieder, and seven Penitential Psalms.

Luca Marenzio (c. 1553-1599) was born in Coccaglio near Brescia, Italy in 1553 or 1554 and is considered to be one of the most prolific and wide ranging madrigal composers of the latter part of the 16th century. The only evidence we have as to Marenzio's date of birth is the statement made by his father, a Brescian notary clerk, that his 35 year old son, Luca, was a musician in the service of the Grand Duke of Florence. Little is know of his early life, but there is evidence that he may have studied with Giovanni Contino in Brescia. He began his musical career in the service of the Cardinal Cristoforo Madruzzo from 1574 to 1578 and was then hired by the Cardinal Luigi d'Este, where he remained until Luigi's death in 1586. It was during his stay with Luigi that Marenzio became internationally known as a composer and produced countless volumes of madrigals that were often reprinted in Italy and published in the north.

After Luigi died it appears that Marenzio eventually was hired into the service of the Grand Duke of Florence, and after this, the number of works that Marenzio wrote became considerably less in number. In fact, nothing was written between the years of 1588 and 1591 and in the last eight years of his life (1591-1599) he only wrote six volumes of madrigals. It is probably that Marenzio was so busy performing and attending to his duties as the music director that he had very little time to write. But for whatever reason, he was never as prolific as he was in the earlier part of his life under the service of the Cardinals in Rome.

Little is known about Marenzio's later years but evidence suggests that he was not close to his patrons and that he moved about freely in musical circles that were connected with the Cardinals residing in Rome. His reputation rests almost exclusively on his secular works, particularly the madrigals, which occupied much of his attention throughout the two decades of his career. His later works are historically significant because of their advanced harmonic procedures. He also wrote about 75 motets. He died in Rome on Aug. 22, 1599. He was known by his contemporaries as the "Divine Composer".

Claudio Monteverdi (c. 1567-1643) was one of the five children born to Baldassare Monteverdi, a distinguished physician. The exact date of his birth has not been confirmed, but he was baptized Claudio Zuan (Giovanni) Antonio on May 15, 1567 in Cremona, Italy. Monteverdi is the spelling as it appears in the signatures of his correspondence to others. In contemporary publications of his works, however, the name is generally spelled Monteverde and there are several other variant spellings. He was an Italian composer of madrigals, operas, and church music and is considered to be one of the key figures in the transition of musical style from the modal music of the Renaissance to the tonal music of the Baroque. In fact, his music contains many modal features but is more tonal in its sound specifically because of his harmonic usage of tones.

Monterverdi was a prolific composer, and his works can be divided into two stylistic periods that coincide with his stays at Mantua (Mantua period) and Venice (Venetian period). In Mantua he was the master of music under the Duke of Mantua and during this time (1590-1612) his life was full of disappointments with critics attacking his works and Monteverdi responding with a number of articles attacking the critics. In the argument between Monteverdi and his critics, the categories of Prima Prattica (old polyphonic style) and Secunda Prattica (modern monodic style) became established. Many of Monteverdi's works from this period have been lost due to political upheavals in Mantua after Monteverdi left to take a post in Venice at St. Mark's Cathedral. It was in the Mantua period that Monteverdi wrote many operas, and his interest was mainly in operatic and madrigal composition during this time.

On Aug. 19, 1613 he accepted the post of Maestro di Capella at St. Mark's Cathedral in Venice. This was the most prestigious and highest paying post in Northern Italy and Monteverdi occupied it for 30 years, during which time his interest quite naturally shifted from opera to church music. However, he continued to write operatic works but the great majority of these have not survived for a variety of reasons.

Monteverdi's importance in the light of posterity is three-fold: he is the last Renaissance composer of madrigals, he is the first composer of performable operas in the sense of early Baroque style, and finally one of the most important composers of church music combining Palestrina's "Stile Antico" (Old Style) with the orchestrally monodistic "Stile Nuovo" (New Style) of the Gabriellis. His works include numerous madrigals, operas, and church music. It is unfortunate that many of his works have been lost forever due to political upheavals and various other reasons. The works that have survived, however, are proof of the extreme importance of this composer in the transition from Renaissance to Baroque.

Thomas Morley (1557-c.1602) A pupil of William Byrd, Morley was organist at St. Paul's Cathedral in 1591 before becoming a gentleman of the Chapel Royal the next year. He was granted a monopoly of music printing but later assigned that to Thomas East in 1600.

Published works include canzonets, madrigals, balletts, consort lessons, and ayres. His Plaine and Easie Introduction to Practicall Musicke (1597) was the first comprehensive treatise on composition printed in England.

Giovanni Pierluigi da Palestrina (c.1525-1594) Giovanni Pierluigi da Palestrina takes his name from his birthplace, Palestrina, a small town near Rome. His entire professional career, from his days as a choirboy at Santa Maria Maggiore to his appointment as "Maestro di cappella" of the Julian Chapel in St. Peter's, was spent in Rome in the service of the church. He has been called "The Prince of Music" and his works are regarded today, as they were in his own day, as supreme examples of the proper liturgical style. Based largely on elements drawn from the Franco-Flemish style, the core of Palestrina's style is imitative counterpoint. The voice parts flow in continuous rhythm, with a new melodic motive for each new phrase of the text. Palestrina's modal melodies, often built on themes from Gregorian chant, are basically stepwise. They have few repeated notes, move within the limited range of a ninth, are easily singable, and exhibit a natural, elegant curve of sound. Harmony, rhythm, and form are also treated with care and restraint; but it is the text which governs the musical organization of his works. His sensitivity to it is evident in his use of pictorial imagery and absolute dedication to proper word accentuation.

Palestrina's works include 92 masses, 600 motets, psalms, hymns, and a number of secular madrigals.

Michael Praetorius (1571-1621) A foremost German composer and theorist, he was one of the most versatile and prolific musicians of his time. Like Hassler, he practiced the elaborate polychoral style of composition cultivated in Venice. In addition to his extensive list of compositional output he wrote three volumes entitled Syntagma musicum, dealing respectively with (1) the origins of liturgical and secular music, (2) a detailed account of instruments and their function, and (3) the notation and methods of performance and principles of choir training in the 17th century.

Thomas Luigi da Vittoria (1548-1611) was born in Avila, Spain and was given the name Tomas Luis da Victoria (Vittoria was the Italianized version of his name). He is considered to be one of the greatest Spanish Renaissance composers. He received his first musical training as a choirboy at the cathedral in Avila and in 1565 he went to Rome to prepare himself for the priesthood. In Rome, his teacher may have been Palestrina, and he was about the same age as Palestrina's two sons. When Palestrinia left his post in the Roman Seminary, Vittoria succeeded him as the Maestro there. In August of 1575, he was ordained a priest, and in 1578, he resigned his post as Maestro at the Seminary and was admitted as a priest to the church of St. Girolamo in Italy where he lived until 1585. In 1583 he dedicated a volume of masses to Philip II and expressed a desire to return to his homeland (Spain).

He returned to Spain in 1587 and was appointed as chaplain to the Empress — Mother Maria, sister of Phillip II, who was living in a convent. He also became the organist and choirmaster of the small church that was part of the convent. When Maria died in 1603, he continued to act as chaplain to her daughter, Margaret, who was a nun at the convent. His last work, a Requiem mass for Maria, is regarded as his most important masterpiece and was published in 1605.

Many of his works were published in his lifetime in Italy and spread all over Europe and the world. He wrote many masses, several volumes of motets, several magnificats, and other church music.

He died in Madrid, Spain on Aug., 1611.

THE BAROQUE PERIOD

THE BAROQUE PERIOD

Major Historical Events

1603	James I crowned King of England
1607	Jamestown (Virginia) settled as the first permanent English colony in North America
1609	Henry Hudson explores the Hudson River
1611	King James translation of the Bible appears
1618	Beginning of the thirty years war
1620	Mayflower docks at Plymouth Rock
1636	Harvard University founded
1648	At five years of age Louis XIV begins rule of France
1653	Oliver Cromwell dissolves Parliament and begins British rule
1660	Charles II is restored as British Monarch
1666	Sir Isaac Newton discovers the Law of Gravity
1692	Salem witchcraft trials
1737	Freemasons established in Germany
1738	John Wesley established the Methodist Church

Music

1600	*Euridice* by Jacopo Peri, the earliest surviving opera. Other important early opera composers were Caccini and Monteverdi
1607	Monteverdi - *Orfeo*
1609	Heinrich Schütz working in Milan
1617	Schütz in Dresden
1637	First public opera house opens in Vienna
1638	Monteverdi - *Madrigals of Love and War*
1642	Monteverdi - *The Coronation of Poppea*
1650	Carissini - *Jephta*
1653	Jean-Baptiste Lully made court composer at Paris
1664	Schütz - *Christmas Oratorio*
1666	Schütz - *St. Matthew Passion*
1669	Paris Academy of Music founded
1676	Birth of Antonio Vivaldi
1681	Arcangelo Corelli writes the first trio sonatas
1685	Birth of Johann Sebastian Bach
1685	Birth of Georg Friedrich Handel
1686	Lully - *Armide*
1703	Handel composing at Hamburg
1704	Bach writes his first cantatas
1706	Handel moves to Italy
1708	Bach working at Weimar
1709	The first piano was built
1710	Handel moves to England
1721	Bach - Brandenberg Concertos, French Suites, English Suites
1722	Bach - *The Well-Tempered Clavier*

1724	Bach - *St. John Passion*
1726	Vivaldi - *The Four Seasons*
1728	Gray - *The Beggar's Opera*
1729	Bach - *St. Matthew Passion*
1733	Pergolesi - *La Serva Padrona*
1734	Bach - *Christmas Oratorio*
1742	Handel - *The Messiah*
1750	Death of J. S. Bach

Visual Arts

1614	Peter Paul Rubens - *The Descent from the Cross*
1624	Franz Hals - *The Laughing Cavalier*
1631	Rembrandt van Rijn - *The Anatomy Lesson*
1634	The Taj Mahal is begun
1642	Rembrandt - *The Night Watch*
1652	Velasquez - *The Maids of Honor*
1678	Bortolome Murillo - *Mystery of the Immaculate Conception*
1735	Hogarth - *A Rake's Progress*
1740	Tiepolo - *Triumph of Amphitrite*

Major Artists of this period were:
Italian: Caravaggio, Bernini, Tiepolo
French: de la Tour, Poussin
Dutch: Rembrandt, Vermeer
Flemish: Rubens, Van Dyck
British: Hogarth
Spanish: El Grecio, Velasquez

Literature

1601	Shakespeare - *Hamlet*
	(Although the works of Shakespeare cross into the Baroque era, his work is still classified as belonging to the Renaissance. The English Renaissance continued into the 17th century.)
1606	Shakespeare - *Macbeth*
1611	King James translation of the Bible
1628	Harvey - *Essay on the Motion of the Heart and the Blood*
1637	Descartes - *Discourse in Method*
1662	Moliere - *Ecole des Femmes*
1667	Milton - *Paradise Lost*
1690	Locke - *An Essay Concerning Human Understanding*
1697	Dryden - *Alexlander's Feast*
1719	Defoe - *Robinson Crusoe*
1723	Voltaire - *Henriade*
1726	Swift - *Gulliver's Travels*
1749	Fielding - *Tom Jones*

Major writers of this period:
English: John Locke, Isaac Newton, Daniel Defoe, John Dryden, John Milton, Jonathon Swift
French: Moliere, Voltaire, Descartes

Musical Style

The term "Baroque" comes from the Portuguese word "barocca" meaning "an irregularly shaped pearl." It is a term borrowed from the fine arts to describe art that was considered (by Renaissance standards) to be "abnormal, bizarre, exaggerated, in bad taste, or grotesque." The art, sculpture, and architecture of this period are considered to be overly decorative, dramatic, flamboyant, and emotional. If Baroque music is compared to Renaissance standards of musical perfection (simplicity, balance, restraint, and refinement), these terms could also be applied to the music of the Baroque. The music is decorative in its use of trills and other forms of musical ornamentation; it is dramatic in its operas, oratorios, and cantatas; it is flamboyant in its attention to the virtuosity of the soloist; and it is emotional in that the moods are musically expressed (sorrow would have a slow moving, drowsy melody broken with many sights and happiness would be a fast moving melody, probably in a major key).

Texture

The move from the Renaissance to the Baroque brought about an important change in the texture of music. In Renaissance music, the melody is supreme, and all musical material comes from the inspiration of the melody. Baroque music centers its attention on the harmony and the function of the harmony. Basically, the change was from a linear or horizontal texture (polyphony) to a vertical texture (homophony). This is not to say that the melody lost its importance in Baroque music; on the contrary, the Baroque melody and the bass line formed the skeleton or outline of musical ideas which could be freely improvised by the performer. The thoroughbass technique (figured bass or continuo), as it was called, employed a kind of musical shorthand. The composer wrote a melody line and a bass line with numbers below the pitches of the bass line. These numbers would tell the performer what harmonies were intended by the composer, and the performer could fill in the harmonies himself. The melody was also slightly improvised through the practice of ornamentation.

Harmony

The transition from the church modes (scales) of the Renaissance to the major-minor system of tonality was one of the most important changes in music history. With a major or minor key center, each chord has a function in relation to that key center. Composers of the Baroque period began to explore the movement from the home key to contrasting keys and back to the home key. This basic three-part harmonic structure led to the eventual shaping of musical forms such as the symphony.

Rhythm

Rhythm in Baroque music takes on major importance. Music of this period has a strong feeling of forward motion. Unlike Renaissance music, Baroque music is metered and thus has regular groupings of strong and weak beats in each measure. For the first time in music history, composers wrote measured music, using time signatures and barlines. The tempo of the music did not change until the very end, thereby strengthening the basic pulse of the music.

Dynamics

Dynamic markings and expressive markings were practically unknown in Baroque music. Dynamic ranges were controlled by the number of players or singers who were asked to perform at one time. Small groups were contrasted with large groups to produce an effect of softer and louder light and shade.

120

Vocal/Choral Music in The Baroque

This period in music history brings about one of the most important changes in direction. It was during the Baroque that composers began writing as much and as often for instruments as they did for voices. Virtually all of European music until the 17th century had been choral music. The great music of the Renaissance is all vocal music. Because of many reasons, instruments now seriously rivalled the voice in amount and quality of repertory.

What are the reasons for this drastic shift? They are many and accumulative reasons, but they could be summarized as:

1) The center of musical activity was no longer only the church and monastery. The Renaissance had seen the rise of the courts of royalty and nobility as major artistic centers. By the 17th century this system of patronage was well in place. Naturally, a composer writing music for a court would not be writing only sacred music, but would write all sorts of music to meet the concert and special occasion needs of the court.

2) The technology of the development of instruments had drastically improved. Many of the standard modern instruments (the violin, the cello, the harpsichord) had become very developed by this time.

3) The aesthetics had changed. Composers became interested in larger, longer forms for pieces. The Renaissance forms were all short forms; rarely would a piece of music last more than five minutes. This was largely due to the fact that the basis for most Renaissance music was a rather brief poem. In the Baroque, composers were no longer primarily interested in setting love poems. They developed a taste for much longer, multi-movement formats for pieces. This direction eventually, though not in the Baroque, led to the full symphony for a large orchestra.

4) The earliest known opera was written in 1600, at the very outset of the Baroque. Before that time there had been very little music written for the solo voice (the troubadours, trouveres and minnesingers of much earlier indicating some of the only excepting). Opera developed very quickly and became very popular. Composers, then, turned a great deal of attention to writing for the solo voice rather than for the choral ensemble. Of course, there was still choral writing done to be included in the context of an opera, just as there is usually a "chorus" in most musical comedies of today.

5) A cappella music for choir became much less common in this period. With numerous newly developing instruments around, and with so many large musical ideas at work, the composers were naturally interested in writing music for chorus with instrumental accompaniments. Besides, this was a relatively new phenomonen; only recently had good, reliable, instruments come on to the scene, and composers wanted to explore the possibilities for combining these instruments with voices.

Opera

The birth of opera in Florence c. 1600 forever changed the history of singing. Suddenly, the individual singer became important. Throughout the 17th century many of our modern vocal techniques were first developed. The first virtuosic singers appeared and began to dazzle the audiences of their time, just as audiences respond to the best opera singers of today.

As mentioned earlier, composers began writing large amounts of instrumental music in the Baroque. The writing for violin particularly advanced very quickly, becoming extremely virtuosic and full of technical display. In a similar fashion, the same sort of writing was done for solo singers. So the development of virtuosic singing techniques and virtuosic playing techniques were closely related, and each influenced the other.

All of this changed the way composers wrote for choirs, and even chorus singers were eventually asked to sing virtuosic lines. The choral music of the Renaissance had certainly made technical demands on singers, but the Baroque composers took this much further. One can think of Handel's Messiah as a good example of this kind of virtuosic writing for choir. The texture of the music has each part, soprano, alto, tenor and bass, performing many fast scales and leaps.

Choirs During The Baroque

Renaissance choirs had been relatively small. In fact, many items in that period there would be just one singer per part. During the Baroque the size of the choir increased, although not usually to the size of our large choirs of today. Still, this was a significant change in choral music. Particularly in pieces with orchestral accompaniment, the choir would need to be large enough to balance the instrumental sound.

As choirs became a little larger, one can imagine that certain issues of choral techniques became more crucial. The more sopranos in a section, the more important the issue of blend becomes. And the more people singing together, the more important it is they execute attacks and releases as an ensemble. Choral ensembles undoubtedly learned from the instrumental ensembles of the period, particularly string ensembles, about making music as a unified ensemble. And instrumental ensembles certainly learned from choral ensembles.

In much of Europe, particularly England, women were still excluded from choirs. The soprano and alto parts were sung by boys with unchanged voices. (This tradition is still kept alive with some choirs today, most noticeably by the British). But women were no longer entirely excluded from singing in ensembles. In the Renaissance court music women certainly had participated. It was generally in sacred music that women had been, and continued to be, excluded. Women opera singers made female participation in music more accepted, and by the end of the Baroque many choirs in Europe, even church choirs were comprised of both women and men.

Choral Music During The Baroque

In the early 17th century the madrigal was still a highly influential type of composition. One development that distinguishes late madrigals as part of the Baroque, rather than the Renaissance, is that composers began to write sets of madrigals to be performed one after the other, all at the same performance. The shorter madrigal of the previoius century was glorified and enlarged, so that many madrigals written as a unified group might be performed as an entire evening's entertainment. Another development is that the form of the madrigals became more varied and complex. They also were very often written to be accompanied by a chamber ensemble of instruments. The most important composer of the early Baroque madrigal was Claudio Monteverdi. His best remembered large madrigal composition is Madrigals of Love and War written in 1638, a piece comprised of many madrigals, all on the same theme, with instrumental accompaniment. A performance of this Monteverdi piece takes nearly two hours, so you can see how times had changed from the short three minute madrigals of 75 years earlier.

In church music, the 17th century was a time of conflict and change. In the Catholic church there were two opposing styles of music: 1) the old, conservative Roman style of Palestrina which had become so well established in the 16th century, and 2) the new "Baroque" style of composition. Both these styles were used throughout the entire Baroque period. Palestrina continued to be upheld as the perfect musical model by some, while others preferred to write in a new style, using a basso continuo as a basis for the clearer harmonies that had emerged. Those writing in Palestrina's style were the only composers of the period devoted to writing exclusively a cappella choral music.

The birth of opera produced a sacred counterpart, the oratorio. These are large, multi-movement pieces very similar to operas in many ways. The text is usually taken from the Bible, though, and sung either in Latin or in the language of the country of the composition (for example, Italian in Italy). There are solo singers who sing arias and duets, and there is also a chorus. The chorus sings movements for chorus alone, or movements in which soloists and chorus sing together. The entire piece is always accompanied by an orchestra which plays a few movements of instrumental music. An important distinction between opera and oratorio is that operas are fully staged with costumes, scenary and acting, while oratorios are performed in a concert setting, without a theatrical production. The most famous oratorio composer of the Baroque is Handel. Most of his oratorios were written when he was living in London, and so they are in English. These pieces typically tell a story of a character or event from the Bible. Handel's most famous oratorio is the Messiah, which tells the story of the life of Jesus. It's still a very popular work and is performed quite often all over the world. The "Hallelujah Chorus" from the Messiah is certainly one of the best known of all classical pieces.

The growth of the Lutheran church in Germany produced church music that was different from the Catholic tradition. One style that had become well established in the 16th century was the chorale. This is usually a four part piece (for soprano, alto, tenor, bass) for unaccompanied choir or for choir with organ accompaniment. The hymns sung in churches today are largely a result of this chorale style. In fact, some hymns from the 16th and 17th centuries are still sung today. The composer who elevated the chorale to its highest possibilities was Johann Sebastian Bach. Bach and Handel are the most prominent of all Baroque composers. Bach wrote hundreds of such chorales to be sung by the choirs and congregation of the church where he worked as choirmaster and organist.

The cantata is a form that arose in the Baroque that is similar to the oratorio. A cantata is written for soloists with or without chorus, accompanied by instruments. These can be either secular or sacred, although we most often think of cantatas as being sacred. Cantatas differ from oratorios in that they are much shorter pieces on a much smaller scale. While an oratorio was probably written to be performed in an opera house or large performing hall or cathedral, a cantata was written for a much more intimate kind of performance in a smaller hall or church. There were many Italians who wrote cantatas in the 17th century: Giacomo Carissimi, Giovanni Legrenzi, Alessandro Stradella, and most notably, Alessandro Scarlatti.

In Germany the cantata did not come into full bloom until the 18th century. These Lutheran church cantatas are similar to those produced by the earlier Italian cantata composers, but with some important differences. The German cantatas were primarily in German, and they also were based on original religious poetry rather than biblical stories. Musically, the German cantata incorporated all the great traditions of the past two centuries: the chorale, the solo song, the contrapuntal "concert" style, instrumental movements, and operatic recitatives and arias. The greatest composer of cantatas of this type was J. S. Bach, who wrote over 200 such works.

Masses continued to be written during the Baroque period, although they are not as prominent as in earlier or later times. Curiously, the most significant mass of the period was written by a non-Catholic. J.S. Bach's Mass in B minor stands as one of the greatest settings of the Latin mass ever composed, and is still part of the standard repertory for choirs of today.

The passion is another important Baroque choral form, perhaps the most important of all Lutheran church music forms. Passions are pieces about the sufferings of Jesus leading up to and through the Crucifixion. In their most mature form, these are large works on the scale of an oratorio. Heinrich Schütz's Seven Last Words is an early example of this type of full-scale passion. As in most other Baroque forms, J. S. Bach distinguished himself as the leading passion composer with works such as the St. John Passion and the St. Matthew Passion.

The motet, first introduced in Gothic times, was still an important Baroque form for chorus, but these 16th and 17th century motets have little resemblance to the motets of the 13th century. At this later time, motets were pieces for chorus in the contrapuntal style without accompaniment, written to biblical or chorale texts. Again, the most shining examples are by J. S. Bach. His six motets are all rather long, multi-movement pieces, the best known Bach motet being Jesu meine Freude (Jesus, My Joy).

The representative works of the Baroque included in the choral repertory of Something New to Sing About are:

"Alleluia" by Bach (TTBB), "Sheep May Safely Graze" by Bach (SAB), "Jesu, Joy of Man's Desiring" by Bach, "I will Extol Thee, My God" by Handel (two part).

Important Baroque Composers

J. S. Bach (1685-1750) inherited a strong family talent and left a significant musical legacy to his many talented children. His long, prolific career began at the age of 15 when he became a choirboy at the Michaeliskirche, Luneburg, where he began organ lessons. An astoundingly significant career followed as such positions as Weimar (where he wrote the bulk of his organ music), Cothen (where he composed a great deal of his secular instrumental works), and his final post as cantor at St. Thomas's, Leipzig, where he composed his enormous amount of church music.

Bach's vast musical output contains every kind of music current at the time, except opera. It was written for practical purposes — for the court orchestra, Sunday services, his sons' instruction, his patrons, and his own use.

Bach was a universal musician, whose music has a universal appeal. It is steeped in the flavor of its period, yet belongs to all time.

George Frideric Handel (Georg Friedrich) (1685-1759) was born in Halle, Germany, the son of a successful barber-surgeon in the court of Saxe-Weissenfels. Although his musical talent surfaced at a very early age, his father did not allow him to practice at the keyboard because he wanted him to become a lawyer. Handel secretly practiced a small clavichord which he smuggled into the attic. Eventually his playing attracted the attention of his father's employer, who convinced his father to allow the boy to study music as well as law. At the age of twelve, Handel became assistant organist of the cathedral in Halle. His musical studies, sponsored by the Duke of Saxe-Weissenfels, included theory, composition, oboe, spinet, harpsichord, and organ.

After a year at Halle University Handel went to Berlin, then to Hamburg as a musician in the opera orchestra. While there he wrote several operas. In 1706 he went to Italy for several years, where he continued to compose. He was associated with the leading patrons and composers of Rome, Florence, Naples, and Venice.

Following a brief return to Germany, he visited England in 1710. He spent the majority of his remaining years in England where he wrote many operas and oratorios as well as some instrumental music. As Director of the Royal Academy of Music, a society organized to promote Italian opera, Handel produced, directed, and wrote oepras. As English audiences grew tired of Italian opera, Handel introduced them to oratorio, a sacred work which is performed without scenery, costumes, or action, but which is dramatic in character and usually is based on biblical events. This form had existed before Handel, but it was really just glorified oepra. Handel changed the structure of the oratorio by giving greater emphasis to the chorus.

Except for a few brief visits to Germany, Italy, and France, Handel remained in England for forty-seven years. He was very popular with British royalty and was the greatest figure in English music during his lifetime. He was buried with public honors in Westminster Abbey. In spite of the total blindness of his last years he continued to play the organ accompaniment for his oratorios. In fact, he played the Messiah a week before his death.

Handel's compositions, both sacred and secular, reveal a spirit of grandeur. Through the immense popularity of his oratorios, he has been recognized as one of the greatest composers of the Baroque age. *Messiah* was his best-known oratorio and is still the most often performed oratorio today.

Henry Purcell (1659-1695) was probably born in London in 1659. He is regarded by many as the greatest English composer of all time. Very little is known of Purcell's personal life, even the identity of his father is uncertain. He married in 1681, had six children, and died leaving his widow very little. Judging by the moral level of some of his tavern songs, Purcell must be regarded as a true child of the Restoration, but his professional life was almost completely linked with the Chapel Royal and Westminster Abbey. He started as a choir boy in the Chapel and rose steadily through the ranks to his final appointment as organist and Gentleman of the Chapel Royal. Purcell undoubtedly received most of his formal education while a chorister at the Chapel, but it is also probable that he was a private pupil of Matthew Locke and John Blow. There is no record of his ever having traveled abroad, and he died in London on Nov. 21, 1695.

The bulk of Purcell's compositions consist of music written for specific occasions involving the royal family and for Chapel and Abbey services. His religious compositions include no less than 60 anthems, five services and many solo songs. Many of the anthems are still sung frequently in England and to some extent elsewhere; the larger verse-anthems are probably the finest examples in this form. Most of his secular compositions were written for the theater; he wrote incidental music for 44 plays and supplied music for six more or less full operas. His most famous composition was *Dido and Aeneas* (c.1689) which is regarded as the first successful English opera. Purcell's importance in the history of English music lies not only in his unusual musical inspiration and freshness, but also in his successful fusing of the more refined continental style with the more rugged idioms of his own country. His sensitive and lucid methods of setting the English language to music have never been equalled. Purcell ws the last great Englishman to carry on the native musical tradition, which was almost completely lost in the continuous flow of foreign fashions to England in the next century.

Heinrich Schütz (1585-1672) was the greatest composer of the middle 17th century, and one of the most important musical figures of the Baroque period. After he began his university studies, Schütz was sent to Venice where he studied with Giovanni Gabrieli from 1609-1612 and brought out his fist published works during this time, a colleciton of five part Italian madrigals. From 1617 to the end of his life, Schütz was master of the Chapel of the Elector of Saxony at Dresden, and during the disturbed times of the thirty years war, he spent several years as court conductor in Copenhagen. Schutz renewed his acquaintances with Italian music when he went to Venice in 1628, especially to meet Monteverdi, whom he greatly admired.

As far as we know, Schütz did not write any independent instrumental works. He is said to have written the first German opera as well as several ballets and other stage works as well, but the music of all of these has been lost. Our knowledge of him, consequently, rests almost entirely on his church compositions of which we possess a considerable quantity and variety. These works date from approximately 1619 to the latest years of his life. The simplest of these works are plain four-part harmonic settings of a German translation of the Calvinist Psalter (1628). He also wrote a considerable amount of Latin motets in which he used a basically more conservative, Catholic, contrapuntal style of composition which is enlivened by certain harmonic novelties and traits derived from the secular madrigal style.

Schütz also wrote several oratorios, the most famous of which are *The Seven Last Words* (1645?) and the *Christmas Oratorio* (1664). These oratorios and his passions are the most significant examples of Lutheran music in the quasi-dramatic form before J.S. Bach.

Antonio Vivaldi (c.1675-1741) was born in Venice about 1675. His father, who was a violinist at St. Mark's Cathedral, was his first teacher and taught the young Vivaldi how to play the Violin. Antonio was ordained a priest in 1703 and from 1704 to 1740 he was the musical director of the Ospendale della Pieta' in Venice, an orphanage which was also one of the famous Venetian music schools for girls. Although he held this post for 36 years, it did not prevent him from traveling and around 1720 he spent three years at Mantua as the Maestro di Capella to Prince Philip of Hesse-Darmstadt. The most important part of his duties in Venice was composition, in which he had great fluency. His enormous output of music includes a large number of operas and some church music. He is better known, however, as a composer of instrumental music, especially concertos, in which he is famed for their lyricism and virtuosity. Very little is known about his life except that he possessed an impulsive personality. Also, because of the reddish color of his hair, he was known as "Il Prete Rosso" or "The Red Priest". In 1740 he left Venice for Cienna as a sick man and died in Vienna the following year.

For a long time, only a very small portion of his musical output was in print, and it is only in recent years that a complete edition of his instrumental works gradually appeared. His works include 73 trio sonatas and 447 concertos, which were written for an astonishing variety of instrumental combinations. Many of them include violins but there are also a considerable amount written for wind instruments. There are also a few written for mandolin and at least one for guitar.

For many years, Vivaldi was remembered simply for the fact that J.S. Bach made several transcriptions of some of Vivaldi's work. But with increased knowledge of his work, he can be appreciated in his own right as a composer who had remarkable power and vitality.

THE CLASSICAL PERIOD

THE CLASSICAL PERIOD

Major Historical Events

1752	Benjamin Franklin discovers electricity
1760	George III rules England
1765	Steam engine invented by Watts
1770	Beginning of the factory system
1776	Declaration of Independence by American colonies
1780	Cornwallis surrenders to Americans at York Town
1789	French Revolution begins
1791	U.S. Bill of Rights ratified
1796	Napoleon begins conquest of Europe
1803	Louisiana Purchase
1804	Napoleon crowned Emperor
1804	Lewis and Clark Expedition
1807	Gas street lamps appear in London
1812	Napoleon retreats from Moscow
1815	Napoleon defeated at Waterloo

Music

1755	Haydn writes his first string quartets
1762	Gluck - *Orfeo ed Euridice*
1764	Mozart meets J. C. Bach in London
1769	Mozart in Italy
1770	Mozart writes his first string quartets
1777	Mozart in Mannheim
1778	La Scala Opera House opens in Milan
1780	Haydn - Quartets, Op. 33
1781	Mozart - *The Abduction from the Seraglio*
1785	Mozart - "Haydn" Quartets
1786	Mozart - *The Marriage of Figaro*
1787	Mozart - *Don Giovanni*
1788	Mozart - *"Jupiter" Symphony*
1789	Haydn - Quartets, Op. 54, 55
1791	Mozart - *The Magic Flute, Requiem*
1791	Haydn's first "London" symphonies
1792	Beethoven moves to Vienna
1798	Haydn - *The Creation*
1799	Beethoven - *First Symphony*
1803	Beethoven - *Third (Eroica) Symphony*
1807	Beethoven - *Fifth Symphony*
1811	Schubert writes his first lieder
1815	Metronome invented

Visual Arts

1770	Gainsborough - *The Blue Boy*
1788	David - *Paris and Helen*
1793	David - *Death of Marat*

Major Artists of the period:
French: Fragonard, David
Spanish: Goya
British: Reynolds, Romney, Gainsborough

Literature

1754	Samuel Johnson - *Dictionary*
1759	Voltaire - *Candide*
1771	*Encyclopedia Brittanica*, first edition
1775	Beaumarchais - *The Barber of Seville*
1781	Kant - *Critique of Pure Reason*
1782	Rousseau - *Confessions*
1784	Beaumarchais - *The Marriage of Figaro*
1790	Kant - *Critique of Judgement*
1798	Wordsworth - *Lyrical Ballads*
1808	Goethe - *Faust, Part I*
1813	Jane Austen - *Pride and Prejudice*

Major Writers of this period:
French: Voltaire, Rousseau, Beaumarchais,
British: Samuel Johnson, William Blake, Jane Austen, Wordsworth
German: Kant, Goethe, Schiller

Musical Style

After about 1750, composers began to write in a new style. In contrast to the contra-puntal, complex texture of Baroque music, the composers of the mid-18th century wanted a simpler, learned, clarified style. They also, whether consciously or not, aimed at creating the first universal European style. When the century had ended, a cosmopolitan style of music had emerged that couldn't really be classified as sounding like any one nationality.

The aesthetic of the time around 1750, was to create noble, yet entertaining music; expressive, yet restrained; natural, and free of needless technical complications. In the early stages the style was extremely simple and light. Johann Christian Bach, a son of J. S. Bach, was the first major composer to emerge in this new style, called stile galant. As the century progressed, the simplicity of these galant beginnings quickly came to full fruition in the development of the sonata form, and the birth of the modern symphony, string quartets and piano sonatas of Haydn and Mozart are the shining end result of the new style.

The Classical period witnessed the most complete development of the patronage system of the arts. Austria and Germany became the undisputed musical centers of Classical music activity. These countries were not governed by a single ruler and therefore still had many small courts which strongly supported the arts. Composers still depended upon the patronage of the courts or of the aristocratic society, but toward the end of the century, the nobility lost some of its wealth and power and could no longer support an entire community of atists and musicians. The concert hall and the opera house were made available to the general public and brought music to the people.

Through technical advances in music printing, music was readily available to amateur musicians. The public interest in music led to increased interest in the history, theory, and practice of music. Public performances were reviewed and critiqued, much as they are today. By the end of the century, music was in the hands of the general public.

Classical Style

One of the most important developments of music in the Classical period was the evolution of clearly defined musical forms. Classical composers organized their music into precise, clear, and well-balanced sections. The most popular formal organization developed from the contrast of two basic melodies, "Melody A" and "Melody B", which were equally balanced to an A-B-A structure. Audiences could easily identify both of the melodies which formed the basis for the development of musical ideas. Music of the Clasical period is identified not only by the symmetry of its formal organization but also by the symmetry of its musical phrases.

Melody

Classical composers placed strong emphasis on the importance of the melody. Classical melodies are generally lyrical and easily singable, utilizing regular four measure phrases. Elements of folk music were gradually introduced into serious music. Audiences could easily recognize familiar folk melodies and rhythms of composers such as Franz Joseph Haydn (1732-1809).

Rhythm

Music of the Classical period uses simple and constant rhythmic patterns which serve to accompany the basic ingredient of the music, the melody. Tempos in Classical music are constant for an entire section and do not slow until the end of a section or a movement.

Silence (long rests) became part of the element of rhythm in Classical music. The ends of sections (cadences) are often followed by an entire measure of rest to clarify or strengthen the cadence.

Harmony

Key signatures were firmly established in the Classical period. The harmony is strongly tonal and generally simple. Classical composers used harmony structurally; that is, formal key relationship between the themes of the movements helped to contrast the musical ideas.

Media

Whereas the Renaissance was mainly a period of vocal music and vocal forms, the Classical period was a time for instrumental forms and instrumental music. Composers wrote music for orchestra, chamber orchestra, solo instruments with orchestra, or music for small groups of instruments. The Classical period was the first to organize the instruments of the orchestra into different groups or families: strings, woodwinds, brasses, and percussion. Each instrumental group was treated as an individual choir.

Instrumental music for small groups (chamber music) became very popular in the Classical period. Music became a performer's art and was widely enjoyed by the general public. Composers began to use expressive markings such as forte (loud) or piano (soft) to indicate their desires to the performers. Dynamic markings were used to build contrast into the music. Tempo markings were also indicated by the composers.

Choral Music During the Classical Period

The late 18th century, or the "Age of Reason" as it is called, was the first era in the Christian age in Europe when the church no longer dominated society, a trend that began taking shape during the Baroque. As a result, not much sacred music was written during these years as compared to earlier times, and virtually all choral music was sacred at this time in history. In a sense, writing for choirs had simply gone out of fashion, for composers were far more interested in writing symphonies, operas, string quartets, keyboard sonatas and all other forms of instrumental chamber works. Nevertheless, the important composers did write a few major works for chorus and orchestra. An interesting feature of the major sacred choral works is that the musical language was now the same for sacred music as it was for secular music. No longer was there a separate style for music of the church. Even the masses composed at this time are in the same musical style and language as the symphonies.

Wolfgang Amadeus Mozart and Franz Joseph Haydn, the two greatest composers of the late 18th century, were close personal friends and each influenced the other in the music they wrote. Each of them wrote several works for chorus and orchestra. These range from "short" masses or mass fragments (for instance, Mozart's *Kyrie in F major*) to full scale oratorios (such as Haydn's *The Creation*). Both of these two men composed large scale masses (such as Mozart's Requiem), works that continue to be regularly performed today. Haydn's two oratorios, *The Creation* and *The Seasons*, are religious works, but not thoroughly biblical. They are of a very restrained religious poetry that reflects the theology and temperament of the times. Certainly Mozart and Haydn both wrote small works for chorus, even just simple part-songs, but they are not significant compared to their enormous instrumental output.

Beethoven was a young man throughout most of what we define as the Classical period. He is difficult to classify as belonging to either the Classical or Romantic period, for he spans both these musical eras. While he decidedly worked in the Classical tradition, his work contains a great deal of the seeds of Romanticism. Like Mozart and Haydn, he did not write many choral works. In fact in all his music there are only three major choral works, two masses (one being the *Missa Solemnis in D*) and the choral finale to his *Symphony No. 9*. Of these the Mass in D and the Ninth Symphony, the two prominent works, belong to his later years and could be considered more to be "Romantic" works rather than "Classical" works. The Mass is almost a symphony itself, set to the Latin mass text, and is a large scale, sprawling work of a size beyond the masses of Haydn and Mozart.

Classical repertory found in the choral collections of Something New to Sing About include "Sing Aloud to God" by Michael Haydn (SSA) (Franz's brother), and "Ecco Quel Fiero Istante" by Mozart (SAB).

Major Classical Composers

Johann Christian Bach (1735-1782) was the youngest son of J. S. Bach and is usually referred to as the "Milan" or "London" Bach due to his extended stays in those two cities. On his fathers death, he went to Berlin to study with his half brother C.P.E. Bach and developed into an outstanding pianist. Opera was his main interest, however, and he managed to travel to Italy which was considered to be the classic land of Opera. He was appointed organist at the Milan cathedral and, in addition, won laurels with his own Operas. His fame quickly spread beyond Italy and in 1761 he was invited to England where he remained for the rest of his life, working as Opera composer, teacher to the

Queen, highly renowned singing and piano instructor to the Aristocracy and conductor of a famous concert series.

His success proved to be too overpowering for him to handle at a comparatively young age and he came to a standstill in his artistic growth. He continued to write music in his earlier style and paid no heed to new trends in music. As a result, he became overshadowed by new persons in the artistic circles and died at the early age of 47, a disillusioned young man. His impact on 18th century music was of the greatest artistic significance in the formation of W. A. Mozart's (considered by many to be the greatest opera composer of all time) style. Johann Christian's influence on Mozart was as decisive as C.P.E.'s influence on Joseph Haydn and in this way the two Bach sons played a vital role in the development of the classical style of music.

J. C. Bach culativated all forms of music known in his lifetime and was equally successful in Vocal and Instrumental composition. His large output includes about 90 symphonies and other works for orchestra; 35 concertos; 120 chamber music works; more than 35 clavier sonatas; 70 pieces of church music; some 90 songs, arias, and cantatas; and 11 operas.

Ludwig van Beethoven (1770-1827) was born in Bonn, Austria. He was one of seven children born to Johann and Maria Beethoven, and he was the oldest of the three surviving sons (several of the seven died in childhood). Ludwig is considered by many to be the greatest composer who ever lived and has been called both a classicist and a romanticist. In reality, he transcends both labels and his music is the expresison of the most powerful musical personalities of all time. He had a childhood of poverty because his father, who was a drunkard, drank away the family's meager income which he (Johann) earned as a singer in the choir at Bonn. His father did, however, teach the young Ludwig the piano and violin so that Ludwig could help increase the family earnings, and tried to force him into a prodigy in imitation of the boy Mozart. In time, the father's salary was increasingly apportioned by his employers to the more talented and dependable Ludwig.

Beethoven's schooling was inadequate, as was his musical instruction aside from the experience of performance. In 1782, he studied with the court organist, Christian Gotrub Neefe, who became Beethoven's first truly capable and methodical teacher. In 1787 he somehow managed a visit to Vienna where he played the piano for Mozart, and Mozart prophesied a great future for the young Beethoven. Ludwig was called back to Bonn because his mother was dying, and he was left with a dependent father and two younger brothers, becoming the sole earner and the head of the family in their struggle for subsistence.

His artistic output is generally divided into three separate and distinct style periods: that of the Vienna years (1792-1802), the second period (1802-1815), and the final years (1815-1827). He came on the scene at a favorable moment in history. He inherited from Mozart and Haydn a style and certain musical forms which were well developed, but still capable of further growth. In the Vienna years, Beethoven was composing music very much steeped in the classical style. These years could be referred to as his learning years, and it was during this time that he studied with Haydn and Albrechtsberger. These were also the years that he also first noticed his loss of hearing. The second period was a time of great growth in his compositions, and it was during this time that he began to show his true genius, achieving a full maturity in his compositions, building on the old styles but increasingly more original and breaking away from the old style. On one occasion a musician asked Ludwig, after a performance of one of his string quartets from this period, if Beethoven considered it to be music, to which Beethoven replied, "the music is not for you, but for a later age." Beethoven wrote some of his most important works during this period, including the *Fifth Symphony*, which is perhaps the world's best known symphony.

It was during the final years that Beethoven became totally deaf. Also during this time he wrote the magnificent "Missa Solemnis" mass and perhaps his longest, most monumental, and mature work, the *Ninth Symphony*. When the *Ninth Symphony* was first performed with its chorale finale in 1824, and with Beethoven standing beside the conductor, the audience was swept away by the mighty summons at its close. They cheered and applauded the composer but he did not turn from facing the orchestra and choir. A singer had to pluck Beethoven's shirt sleeve and direct his attention to the audience before he bowed to an ovation he could not hear. Beethoven died on March 22, 1827 in Vienna. A multitude of people, aware that a great artist had left them, followed an elaborate funeral procession. Never before in the history of music had such public homage been paid to a musician.

His works include nine symphonies, eleven overtures, incidental music to plays, 16 string quartets, 30 piano sonatas, nine piano trios and other chamber works, ten violin sonatas, five cello sonatas, an oratorio, an opera (*Fidelio*), two masses, and a number of arias, songs and numerous lesser compositions of different sorts. All of these works anticipated or created trends that continued throughout the 19th century, and his works remain among the greatest and most loved compositions ever written.

Christoph Willibald Gluck (1714-1787) was born in Erasbach, Austria on July 2, 1714 in an area that is now part of present day Czechoslovakia. He was probably of Czech origin and he spent the early part of his life studying in what is now Czechoslovakia. In 1732, he went to Prague where he may have studied at the university, but certainly supported himself by singing in church choirs and playing the violin and cello. He is also thought to have studied with various musicians during this stay in Prague. In 1736 he went to Vienna where he was hired by the Prince Melzi and moved to Milan where he studied for three years with Sammartini. It was during this time that he wrote his first opera and thereafter led the life of a successful Italian composer. He wrote operas that were performed in many of the artistic cities of the time such as Venice, Milan, Bologna, and Turin. In 1745 he traveled to London via Paris and it was in Paris that he heard an opera by J.P. Rameau. While in London he met with G.F. Handel and other English composers of his time.

It was during these years that Gluck was still learning the craft of writing operas and it wasn't until several years later that he finished his first true masterpieces (*Orfeo ed Euridice* and *Alceste*). From this point on, Gluck wrote many operas and stage music and came to be known as the "Father of Modern Day Opera." He wrote in both the "serious" Italian style of opera, and the "lighter" style of the French Opera Comique.

Gluck belonged entirely to his age, and his mature masterpieces are the epitome of that 18th century classicism which was being superseded even in his lifetime by the ideals and emotions of the young romantic movement. His best works survive today on the margin of the operatic repertory, thanks to their noble simplicity and dramatic force.

Franz Joseph Haydn (1732-1809) was born in Rohrau of lower Austria on March 31, 1732 or perhaps April 1; the sources are not quite clear. He showed promise as a musician at a very early age, singing songs with his father very much in tune. When he was seven years old, he went off to Vienna to study at St. Stephen's Cathedral and remained a soprano in the choir there until he was 18 years old, at which time his voice began to change and he turned to learning the craft of musical composition. In 1757 he received an invitation from Count Furnberg to spend a summer at his castle in Weinzierl, and it was here that Haydn invented the String Quartet as we know it today (two violins, viola, and cello). Two years later he accepted a post as music director for Count Morzin in Bohemia, and it was under his patronage that he wrote his first symphonies. This relationship lasted two years and Count Morzin had to release all his musicians due to financial difficulties. At this time Haydn accepted an invitation to become Vice Kapellmeister in the court of Prince Paul Esterhazy in May of 1761 and remained in the service of the Esterhazy family for over 45 years.

An interesting story about Haydn's "Farewell Symphony" is due to the long stays that musicians had at the Ezterhazy summer castle. In the summer, the musicians were obliged to remain with the Prince at the Esterhazy summer castle for as long as the Prince stayed and, except for Haydn and the Leader of the Orchestra, were not allowed to bring their families with them. In 1772, when the Prince had stayed on longer than usual at the summer castle, the musicians begged Haydn to write a piece that would suggest to the Prince that it was time to go back home to Vienna. Haydn responded by writing the "Farewell Symphony" in which, during the last movement, one player after another finishes and walks off the stage until there are only two solo violins left (these were Haydn and the Leader). The Prince watched with astonishment as his Kapellmeister and leader blew out their candles and prepared to depart. The story goes that the Prince got the point and the court left for Vienna the next day.

In the winters, when Haydn was in Vienna, he became friendly with W. A. Mozart and each composer admired the other and would not tolerate a bad word said against his friend. Mozart and Haydn learned a great deal from each other, and their friendship was certainly one of the most fruitful in the history of music. According to Haydn's own testimony, Mozart affectionately referred to Haydn as "Papa" as did the orchestra members at Esterhazy castle and the name has stuck down through the ages. The term "Papa" was originally one of respect and admiration, but came to be used condescendingly in later years.

On his return trip to Austria in the summer of 1792, Haydn met Ludwig van Beethoven at Bonn and accepted him as a pupil. Haydn immediately saw the genius of Beethoven and wrote in 1793 that "he will one day be considered one of Europe's greatest composers and I shall be proud to be called his teacher." Some of Haydn's greatest works were written in the final years of his life (the last symphonies #100-106), the oratorios (*The Creation* and *The Seasons*), and his last 6 masses are among his finest works. He died during the night of May 31, 1809 in his sleep and was buried two days later with very few people in attendance.

It is impossible to determine exactly how many compositions Haydn wrote because many publishers of the day put his name on many works because it would sell copies. Provisionally, the list of authenticated compositions include 106 symphonies; 68 string quartets, numerous overtures, concertos, divertimentos, serenades, Baryton trios, string trios, piano trios and other chamber works, 60 piano sonatas, songs, arias, cantatas, masses, and other settings of liturgical texts, between and 25 operas and four oratorios.

Haydn's position in the history of music has been established on several grounds. He was a tireless innovator and together with Mozart and Beethoven, he formed and brought to a rare degree of perfection, the so-called Vienna classical school. The beginnings of his style are in the receding baroque era, and his late period style leads us almost straight into the Romantic era. In the 50 years of his creative life, he spanned an almost immeasurable stylistic gap from Bach to Beethoven. The 19th century concentrated its attention on Bach and Beethoven, and tended to forget the giant who bridged the two eras. Without Haydn, the history of music would perhaps have taken on an entirely different course.

Wolfgang Amadeus Mozart (1756-1791) was born in Salzburg, Austria on January 27, 1756 and is considered by many to be one of the world's greatest musical geniuses. His father, Leopold, was a well-known composer and theorist who noticed Wolfgang's talent when Wolfgang was very young (Wolfgang was only 3 years old when he began to play tunes at the harpsichord which he had heard). At the age of five, Mozart began to write Minuets for the harpsichord which his father notated. In January of 1762, when Mozart was just six, Leopold took his 2 children (Wolfgang and his older sister - Maria Anna, also known as "Nannerl") on tour to play for many of the crowned heads of Austria and Germany. This touring lasted for 10 years and Leopold and his son were in Salzburg barely 3 of those 10 years. From 1763 until 1766 the Mozarts extensively toured Europe including Brussels and Paris. Eventually, Mozart played for many of the crowned heads of all Europe, countless Bishops, Archbishops, and Cardinals and was even received by Pope Clement XIV on July 8, 1770 where he was presented the "Order of the Golden Spur" to which was attached the title "Cavaliere". He studied composition with some of the greatest composers of the day including Johann Christian Bach, Padre Martini, and Giovanni Battista Sammartini. He later studied and befriended Joseph Haydn, who once told Mozart's father "Your son is the greatest composer I know either personally or by reputation," which was an extremely great compliment coming from one of the greatest composers of the day.

There has never been a composer who wrote so brilliantly for so many different media as did Mozart. Mozart was equally at home writing Symphonies (41 in all), Concertos (his piano concertos are still considered to be some of the best ever written), divertimentos, string quartets and quintets, operas, masses, sonatas, or trios. In fact, next to J. S. Bach, Mozart is the most prolific composer (writing over 600 works in all) in the common practice period, which is particularly astounding when you consider that Mozart only lived to be 35 years old. As with many artists, Mozart did not achieve the fame and fortune he so rightly deserved during his lifetime, but to this day his popularity and respect as a composer is equalled only by Bach and Beethoven. Early in 1791, when Mozart was already a sick man, a stranger in a gray suit appeared and commissioned him to write a Requiem Mass. Mozart believed that he was writing his own Requiem and worked feverishly on the score until he dropped from exhaustion. On the evening of December 4, 1791, he died. He had amassed many debts and had little money when he died, so he was buried in a Pauper's grave, the exact location of which has never been discovered.

If there is one medium of composition in which Mozart excelled (although he wrote well in all), it would be opera. His operas are considered among the greatest ever written and many feel there will never be another equal to Mozart in the writing of opera. The most famous of his many operas are *The Abduction from the Seraglio, The Marriage of Figaro, Cosi Fan Tutti, The Magic Flute*, and *Don Giovanni*.

ROMANTICISM

ROMANTICISM

Major Historical Events

1819	First steamship across the Atlantic
1821	The electric motor and generator are invented
1823	Monroe Doctrine
1830	First railroad, Liverpool to Manchester, England
1837	Morse invents the telegraph
1837	Queen Victoria crowned
1838	Birth of photography, Daguerre takes the first photographs
1840	Incandescent light bulb invented
1846	Smithsonian Institute founded
1848	Gold Rush in California
1859	Charles Darwin writes Origin of the Species
1861	Civil War in the United States
1861	Unification of Italy
1863	Lincoln gives Gettysburg Address, Emancipation Proclamation
1867	Purchase of Alaska from Russia
1869	Suez Canal opens
1869	First American transcontinental railroad
1876	Bell invents the telephone
1877	Edison invents the phonograph
1881	Panama Canal built
1886	Statue of Liberty in New York Harbor
1888	Kaiser Wilhelm II crowned in Germany
1895	Wilhelm Roetgen discovers X-rays
1898	Spanish American War

Music

1816	Rossini - *The Barber of Seville*
1822	Beethoven - *Missa solemnis*
1822	Schubert - *Unfinished Symphony*
1827	Death of Beethoven
1829	Berlioz - *Symphonie Fantastique*
1835	Donizetti - *Lucia di Lamermoor*
1836	Chopin - *Ballades*
1843	Wagner - *The Flying Dutchman*
1846	Mendelssohn - *Elijah*
1848	Stephen Foster begins writing songs
1851	Verdi - *Rigoletto*
1854	Liszt - *Piano Sonata in B minor*
1859	Wagner - *Tristan und Isolde*
1867	First collection made of Negro Spirituals
1868	Brahms - *A German Requiem*
1874	Verdi - *Requiem*
1875	Bizet - *Carmen*

1881	Boston Symphony founded
1885	Gilbert and Sullivan - *The Mikado*
1888	Tchaikovsky - *Fifth Symphony*
1889	Richard Strauss - *Don Juan*
1893	Humperdinck - *Hansel and Gretel*
1896	Puccini - *La Boheme*
1897	Sousa - *Stars and Stripes Forever*
1899	Sibelius - *Finlandia*

Visual Arts

1821	Constable - *The Hay Wain*
1838	Delacroix - *The Capture of Constantinople*
1839	Turner - *The Fighting Temeraire*
1849	Courbet - *The Stone Breaker*
1857	Currier and Ives prints
1863	Manet - *Olympia*
1873	Degas - *Place de la Concorde*
1877	Monet - *Care Saint-Lazare*
1884	Seurat - *Sunday Afternoon on Grande Jatte*
1888	Van Gogh - *The Sunflowers*
1889	Eiffel Tower completed
1889	Rodin - *The Thinker*
1892	Toulouse-Lautrec - At the Moulin Rouge

Major artists of the period:
British: Constable, Turner
French: Delacroix, Courbet, Manet, Monet, Degas, Rousseau, Renoir, Seurat, Toulouse-Lautrec, Gaugin, Ingres, Rodin
Dutch: Van Gogh
American: Whistler, Cassatt

Literature

1816	Shelley - *Alastor, or the Spirit of Solitude*
1817	Byron - *Manfred*
1819	Scott - *Ivanhoe*
1826	Cooper - *The Last of the Mohicans*
1836	Dickens - *The Pickwick Papers*
1839	Poe - *Tales of the Grotesque and Arabesque*
1844	Dumas - *The Three Musketeers*
1848	Marx - *Communist Manifesto*
1849	Dickens - *David Copperfield*
1850	Hawthorne - *The Scarlet Letter*
1851	Melville - *Moby Dick*
1852	Stowe - *Uncle Tom's Cabin*
1854	Thoreau - *Walden*
1855	Whitman - *Leaves of Grass*
1864	Carroll - *Alice in Wonderland*
1864	Tolstoy - *War and Peace*
1866	Dostoyevsky - *Crime and Punishment*
1867	Ibsen - *Peer Gynt*

1869	Verne - *Twenty Thousand Leagues Under the Sea*
1876	Twain - *Tom Sawyer*
1883	Stevenson - *Treasure Island*
1884	Twain - *Huckleberry Finn*
1891	Doyle - *Adventures of Sherlock Holmes*
1893	Crane - *The Red Badge of Courage*

Major Writers of the period:

British: Shelley, Byron, Scott, Austen, Dickens, Wilde, Longfellow, Carroll, Browning, Doyle, Tennyson, Kipling

French: Balzac, Hugo, Dumas, Flaubert, Baudelaire, Maupassant, Proust, Verlaine

Russian: Tolstoy, Pushkin, Dostoyevsky, Chekov

Other Europeans: Strindberg, Ibsen, Nietzche, Kierkegaard

American: Twain, Poe, Dickinson, Whitman, Stowe, Melville, James, Emerson

Beginnings of Romanticism

Romanticism as a movement probably began with the literature of the 18th century, particularly with such writers as Rousseau and Goethe. In contrast to the restraint and objectivity of their artistic climate, these writers and others turned to a much more personal approach to art. The individual's emotions were the focus rather than more objective intellect. The French and American Revolutions were part of this change in outlook, for in both those cases the thrust was the rights of the individual and the overthrow of the ruling class. By 1800 the political climate of the entire European scene had so changed that the courts and aristocracy, so long in total control of society, had begun to drastically fade, and the middle class, the bourgeoisie, had begun its rise to prominence in western society.

Romantic Music

Music, for whatever reason, tends to be slightly behind literature and politics in times of major shifts in society. The classical tradition was still in place in the early 19th century although there were certainly clues that changes were brewing. The musician's place in society until that time had largely been one of an honored servant. With few exceptions, most composers had been in the service of either the church or the court as contracted employees, largely providing music to meet the needs of the clery or royalty. Prior to the romantic movement, the glorified musical celebrity was largely an unknown, undefined phenomenon. At the rise of Romanticism, the musician's place in society changed almost entirely. The most important audience for the composer became the concert-going middle class, not the royalty or clergy of earlier times. The individual musician, or artist of any type, now had a wide range of possible futures, he could become a widely successful celebrity, could die in obscurity, or could have some degree of moderate success between those two extremes. Without the court or church as patron, musicians had to make their own way by either winning over concert going audiences, or, failing to do so, live in poverty. Our modern concept of the "artist" was now born in both its extremes: 1) the much adored famous personality, made rich by the continuing interest of international audiences because of the appeal of a unique individual flair, and 2) the starving artist hard at work in a cold attic, nobly suffering, living in obscurity, but discovered after death to be enormously talented. Such "romanticized" notions were born in the 19th century and are still with us today.

The radical changes in the music representative of the 19th century were in part made possible by the sweeping changes in the moral, political, and social climate of the age. First, the Industrial Revolution had a direct reflection on the orchestras of the 19th century: (1) the instruments were mass-produced and therefore cheaper and more readily available; (2) the instruments were greatly improved (the addition of valves to the brass instruments and the iron-cast frame and thicker strings on the piano), and performers could better accommodate the composer's requirements for emotional expression. Second, the gradual change from an aristocratic society to a democratic society brought with it previously unavailable opportunities for the middle class. More and better-trained musicians gave the composers the talent necessary to render their creations. Public concerts in concert halls necessitated an increase in the size and scope of the orchestra—the acoustics of the hall demanded greater flexibility in musical expression.

Composers of the 19th century were interested in communicating directly with the conductor or performer; thus a characteristic vocabulary of expressive terms emerged to indicate not only tempo but also mood: "dolce" (sweetly), "cantabile" (in a singing manner), "maestoso" (majestic), "dolente" (weeping), "con passione (with passion)," "con fuoco" (with fire), "con amore" (with love, tenderly).

Nationalism was an important influence in Romantic music. The composer used folk songs, folk dances, and legendary folk heroes to identify his music with his native land. Nationalism, which grew out of a reaction against the musical supremacy of the Germans (Bach, Beethoven and Brahms) and the long tradition of Italian, English, and French music, was prominent in the music of such European nations as Russia, Finland, Norway, and Spain that were without established national traditions of their own.

Instrumental music during this century grew in size and scope, until, by the end of the century, a symphony orchestra might number one hundred players. The classical forms of pieces were still written, but now they often had descriptive titles. Pieces were written to evoke a dramatic scheme, or to tell a story in music, such as Berlioz's *Symphonie Fantastique*. Piano music was particularly popular, and many composers/performers specialized in music for the piano, such as Clementi, Chopin and Liszt.

Opera continued to be an important musical form. In the first part of the century a style of extremely virtuosic singing came out of Italy, called *bel canto*, in which the singer would dazzle audiences with amazing technical displays. The operas of Rossini, Donizetti and Bellini are in this style, along with the early operas of Verdi. As the century progressed, styles of singing changed. Giuseppe Verdi's mature works are for a much larger voice than the lighter voices so popular at the beginning of the century. Perhaps the most important composer of the entire 19th century was Richard Wagner of Germany, who wrote operas exclusively. Not only did Wagner make enormous demands in singers, writing for only the largest, fullest voices demanded to sing over huge orchestral sounds, but he also changed forever the concepts of harmony by enlarging the scope of chromaticism. By the end of the century many of the composers in Europe were following Wagner's example in trying to create heroic music of enormous proportions. It was certainly a striking contrast to the restraint and balance of 100 years earlier; the aesthetic climate had changed.

One of the most important developments in the vocal music of the 19th century was the evolution of the accompanied art song, the "lied" (German, for song). The great lyric poetry of the age (Goethe, Schiller, Heine) was combined with the solo voice and the piano to produce a highly personal and subjective musical expression. The lied attained its greatest height in the music of the gifted composer, Franz Schubert (1797-1828), whose 600 songs stand as the most expressive examples of this form. Schubert's songs reveal his unmatched supremacy in creating beautiful melodies, but it must not be inferred that Schubert was famous only for his songs. Indeed, he was a leading composer of the 19th century and in his brief life of 31 years created masterpieces for orchestra, small instrumental ensembles, piano, and choir. Other German composers who contributed significantly to the lieder repertoire were Robert Schumann (1810-1856), Johannes Brahms (1833-1897), and Hugo Wolf (1860-1903).

Choral Music of The 19th Century

The choral music of the 19th century falls into three main categories:

1. Part songs or short choral pieces in which the composer uses the chorus as the main focal point. Songs are performed either a cappella or accompanied by piano or organ. Important composers: Johannes Brahms, Felix Mendelssohn, Robert Schumann, Franz Schubert, Hugo Wolf, and Gabriel Faure.

2. Music with liturgical texts that are written for use in the church. Important composers: Franz Schubert, Felix Mendelssohn, Luigi Cherubini, Charles Gounod, Dimitri Bortniansky, Johannes Brahms, and Gabriel Faure.

3. Music for chorus and orchestra (with or without soloists) that is intended for performance in a concert hall. Important composers: Hector Berlioz, Gioacchino Rossini, Giuseppe Verdi, Anton Bruckner, Johannes Brahms.

Important Composers of The Period

Johannes Brahms (1833-1897) was the son of Johann Jakob Brahms, a double bass player, and Johanna Henrika Christiane Nissen—17 years older than her husband. Johannes began studying piano when he was seven. His teacher quickly realized his great talent and referred him to his own teacher, Eduard Marxsen who was an expert on Bach and Beethoven. When Johannes was thirteen he was studying theory, and a tour to America as a prodigy had already been discouraged forhis greatest growth. He earned money during this time by composing short compositions as well as playing in taverns.

When he was 20 he went on tour as an accompanist to a Hungarian violinist, Eduard Remenyi. He was introduced to Liszt who was impressed by Brahm's compositions. He met and became a close friend with Joachim, also a violinist. Soon parting from Remenyi, he set out on a walking tour in Rhineland and presented himself at Schumann's home in Dusseldorf. Schumann welcomed him, encouraged him, helped publish some works, and wrote about him in his music journal. He went home briefly before being recalled to Dusseldorf concerning Schumann's breakdown. The next two years were spent there and he became deeply devoted to Clara Schumann. Schumann died in 1856, and Brahms remained in touch with Clara for the rest of her life.

For a few years he taught at the court of Detmold, and also in Hamburg. In 1859 he was appointed conductor of a ladies' choir and wrote a great deal of choral music. His last thirty years were spent in and around Vienna, composing *Academic Festival Overture*, four symphonies, Piano Concerto No. 2 (one of the most difficult in the repertoire), *Liebeslieder* Waltzes (Love-Song Waltzes), and the *Deutsches Requiem* (German Requiem).

Because of his highly crafted pieces using counterpoint (complex, imitative techniques such as canon and fugue), and the variation process, Brahms has earned world respect as the last of the three B's—Bach, Beethoven, and Brahms.

Suggested Listening: *Academic Festival Overture*
Symphony No. 3
"How Lovely Is Thy Dwelling Place"from the *German Requiem*

Frederic Chopin When one thinks of the piano, one name immediately comes to mind: Chopin, called "the poet of the piano". Frederic Chopin (pronounced sho-pan) was born near Warsaw, Poland, on March 1, 1810. He was the second of four children, and the only son of a poor Frenchman who emigrated to Poland to avoid the draft. The father, Nicolas, taught French to earn his keep in Poland, and married a poor relation of a family in which he tutored.

In contrast to many child prodigies, Chopin received a good, well-rounded education. He was precocious, writing verses at six. Musically he was practically self-taught, although he was kept in bounds by the discipline of a teacher, Adalbert Zwyny, who had him study the music of Johann Sebastian Bach and the Viennese masters. He composed small pieces and improvised often, already using his favored black-note key, G-flat. When he was seven years old, a court band played a march of his, and he appeared in concert playing a piano concerto when he was eight.

In high school, Chopin studied with Joseph Elsner, director of the Warsaw Music Conservatory, and now had systematic instruction in music theory—harmony and counterpoint—and form. He was quite successful playing, as Mozart had, before the nobility, who presented him with trinkets and jewels.

When he was nineteen he set off for Vienna and was quite successful in his concerts there, largely because of his improvisations on Polish folk tunes—something exotic for the Viennese audiences. Upon his return to Poland he spent his time writing his two famous piano concertos, both of which contain a last movement in Polish dance-form. Although he was anxious to return to Vienna, he was delayed in Poland due to the Polish rebellion against Russian domination, a delay also encouraged by his infatuation with a young singing student at the Conservatory, Constantia Gladkowska. The slow movement of the F minor Concerto (No. 2) is said to have been inspired by his feelings for her.

On a second trip to Vienna in 1830-31, he attracted the attention fo the famous composer Robert Schumann, who wrote of Chopin in his musical newspaper column: "Hats off, gentlemen! A genius!" Unable to return home because of the war, Chopin toured Europe. Saddened by the news of the capture of Warsaw by the Russians, he wrote the famous "Revolutionary" Etude in C minor, Op. 10, No. 12. Chopin's music was becoming respected for such things as the Polish folk element, the singing quality of his music (in such mood pieces as his Nocturnes), and brilliant virtuosity (in such pieces as his Etudes and Polonaises). His glittering passage work stretched the pianist's dexterity to its limits, yet his melodies were lyrical enough that even today popular songs are made from them.

Chopin made his way to Paris and there became acquainted with the great men of the time, Liszt, Bellini, Berlioz and Meyerbeer. But his delicate sensitive piano playing could not compete with bombastic giants like Liszt and Thalberg, and Chopin virtually retired from public performing to teach piano privately. Chopin also became acquainted with many famous writers and artists in the Paris literary circles, and gradually found himself drawn to the novelist Aurore Dupin, who published under a masculine name, George Sand. Because Chopin had been ill with tuberculosis, he and George Sand traveled in 1838 to the island of Majorca in search of a healthier climate. (While there he wrote the 24 Preludes, which are often played by piano students.) Both his physical condition and the relationship with Sand deteriorated and Chopin returned to Paris alone. The final parting of the lovers occurred in 1847. Chopin tried a brief concert tour to England and resumed teaching, but he was too ill. His attempts to contact George Sand were in vain, and he died alone in Paris in 1849. At his own request his heart was sent to his beloved Warsaw for emtombment.

Suggested Listening: Piano Concerto No. 2 in F-minor, Op. 21, slow (Larghetto) movement
"Revolutionary" Etude in C minor, Op. 10, No. 12
Preludes, Op. 28, Nos. 4, 7, 15,

Stephen Foster was an early pioneer of American folk music. He was born, patriotically, on July 4, 1826 in Lawrenceville, Pennsylvania. His father was a businessman, and

142

mayor of Allegheny City. His mother described him as unique among her eight children, because at six he was playing the flute and writing music. When he was thirteen he composed a waltz for flute quartet. At eighteen he published his first song "Open Thy Lattice, Love". At twenty he became a bookkeeper for his brother in Cincinnati (one brother helped build up the Pennsylvania Railroad), but his composing was more important and he returned home. In 1850 he married Jane MacDowell, a soprano who enjoyed singing Foster's songs at family gatherings. They moved to New York and had a daughter, but the marriage was not happy and Foster returned home to Pittsburgh.

Foster's "Old Folks at Home", often known as "Swanee River" because the first line is "Way down upon de Swanee ribber", was published and used by E. P. Christy in his traveling minstrel company in 1851. Interestingly, Foster never saw the South and found the name of the Swanee River in a book. Other minstrel songs he wrote were "Old Black Joe", "My Old Kentucky Home" and "Camptown Races". He appealed to the society set with "Jeanie With the Light Brown Hair", "Come Where My Love Lies Dreaming", and "Beautiful Dreamer". During the Civil War he wrote "Willie We Have Missed You", and "Massa's in de Cold, Cold Ground". All together, he wrote some 189 songs and received a fair income from them, but he became an alcoholic and a drifter in New York, and squandered his money. He died penniless in the charity ward of Bellevue Hospital in 1864 at the age of 38.

Suggested Listening: "Old Folks at Home" (Swanee River)
"Old Black Joe"
"My Old Kentucky Home"
"Camptown Races"
"Jeanie With the Light Brown Hair"

Franz Liszt (pronounced List) was perhaps the greatest piano performer or virtuoso of all time. For many years he was idolized by all of Europe as much as any rock or pop star of today.

He was born in Raiding, Hungary, in 1811. His father, a steward in the employ of Prince Esterhazy, instructed Liszt in piano. He appeared in public recital at age nine, and as a result, some Hungarian noblemen financed his musical studies for six years. At eleven he went to Vienna and performed in public, to much acclaim. When he was twelve, Beethoven attended one of his concerts and kissed him on the forehead. Liszt studied piano with Czerny and compositoin with Salieri (colleague of Mozart and teacher of Schubert).

In 1823 he went to Paris hoping to study at the Paris Conservatory. But Cherubini, the director, who disliked child prodigies, refused him entrance, using the excuse that he was a foreigner. Liszt stayed on studying privately. When Liszt's father died, the 16 year old was already well-known as a virtuoso, and could support himself and his mother. He moved in the literary circles, making friends with the great Victor Hugo and George Sand
. In 1830 Liszt saw Paganini's spectacular violin performances, and determined to have a similar dramatic career. He began to explore the possibilities of the piano and launched a virtuoso career. He developed eccentric mannerisms. He began wearing white gloves, which he elaborately removed in front of the audience. He also began to improvise on themes provided by the audience.

He lived with the Countess D'Agoult during this time, and the oldest of their children, Cosima, eventually became famous as the wife of Wagner. Liszt began to help other less fortunate composers such as Wagner. He championed many new works of other composers and was in the forefront of experimentation himself. He created a new form—the symphonic poem—and wrote *Les Preludes* in this style. He experimented with new scales, such as the one made of whole-tones, and new chords (in the Faust Symphony), and produced extremely difficult piano works, such as the B minor Sonata for piano, the Mephisto Waltz, and the *Etudes d'execution transcendental* (Transcendental Etudes) which are virtually impossible to play and rarely performed because of their difficulty.

After years as a concert idol, Liszt became a minor priest in the Catholic Church and spent his old age helping other musicians.

Suggested Listening: *Les Preludes*
       Mephisto Waltz
       Hungarian Rhapsody No. 2

Felix Mendelssohn. A happy combination of great talent and family wealth provided Felix Mendelssohn with the good fortune for which every composer wishes. Felix was born in Hamburg, Germany in 1809. His father was a banker, his grandfather the famous philosopher Moses Mendelssohn. His mother Leah taught her four children music, art, literature, and foreign languages. As the children grew, their parents continued to provide the best instruction. The Mendelssohn home in Berlin soon became a musical center. Felix played piano, organ and viola, and conducted a young orchestra he assembled to play his own music for Sunday morning gatherings. Carl Friedrich Zeltler, Felix's teacher, early recognized his talent and took him to meet the great German writer Goethe (pronounced Gur-ta) as well as famous musicians. He performed in public at the age of 9 and wrote very mature pieces during his teens. At 17 he wrote a remarkable piece, the Overture to Midsummer Night's Dream, still a concert favorite today. The joyous wedding march from this work is the one still traditionally used by the bridal party as they exit the ceremony.

Mendelssohn provided a historical moment when he conducted Bach's *St. Matthew Passion in 1829,* an event which began a revival of the composer's virtually forgotten vocal music. He formed a Bach Society, and supervised an edition of Bach works.

Mendelssohn himself was acclaimed as a fine pianist and conductor, and toured England. His *Fingal's Cave Overture* depicts the sea sounds he remembered from his visit. The "Scotch" and "Italian" Symphonies were also the results of his travels.

Other famous compostions were his Violin Concerto, probably the most famous one written, the group of piano pieces called *Songs Without Words*, and the sacred oratorio Elijah. Although he died an early death at 38, Mendelssohn's place in history is assured because of his compositons, his teaching at the Leipzig Conservatory which he founded, and especially his re-discovery of Bach.

Suggested Listening: Overture to *Midsummer Night's Dream* and Wedding March
       Violin Concerto
       "Italian" Symphony

Giacomo Puccini "The most popular opera composer in the world". It would be hard to deny that claim for Giacomo Puccini (pronounced poo-chee-nee), though as a child he showed no interest or talent! When he was born in 1858 in Lucca, Italy, there was already a long family tradition of prominent musicians, so he was sent early to a music school. He made good progress as a pianist and organist, but was 22 years old before he was able financially, with the aid of a grant from Queen Margherita of Italy, to go to the best music school, the Milan Conservatory. At the urging of his teacher, Ponchielli, he began to write operas, but achieved no real success until he wrote Manon Lescaut in 1893. It was a triumph when it was produced in Turin. His next opera, *La Boheme* (The Bohemians) was even more of a triumph. The story of a group of young artists and musicians trying to survive in Paris was similar to Puccini's own struggle to eat and keep warm as a poor student. Shortly, those hard times were gone. Puccini became quite famous and wealthy, ironically, because of a series of operas depicting hardship. *Tosca* (1900) concerns a young woman's sacrifice for her lover, and *Madama Butterfly* (1904) tells of a young Japanese woman's rejection by an American sailor. *Madama Butterfly* was booed and hissed at its premiere, but soon gained enormous popularity. Both operas end in the tragic suicide deaths of the heroines. All three of his most famous operas (*La Boheme*, *Tosca*, and *Madama Butterfly*) were written in a short ten-year period, and have become three of the most popular operas world-wide.

His other famous operas include one on an American subject, *The Girl of the Golden West*, and a set of three one-act operas, known as the *Trittico*: *Il Tabarro*, *Suor Angelica* (Sister Angelica, concerning nuns in a convent), and *Gianni Schicchi*. *Gianni Schicchi* is particularly popular with its comic situations and all's-well ending.

Puccini's operas are known for their beautiful melodies, and audiences typically leave the performance humming them. Puccini's operas are usually the first favorites of students.

Puccini died of cancer in 1924 before he could finish *Turandot*, an exotic opera with oriental setting. He was given a state funeral—most fitting for a composer who brought such glory to Italian opera.

Suggested Listening: Excerpts from *La Boheme*
Excerpts from *Tosca*
Excerpts from *Madama Butterfly*

Gioacchino Rossini. It may seem strange that a reluctant composer could have a major impact on history, but that is the case with Gioacchino Rossini (pronounced row-see-nee). He was blessed with musical abundance even at birth (1792)—his mother was an opera singer, his father a town trumpeter in Pesaro, Italy. Blessed later with good looks and a beautiful voice, Rossini was a choir boy at age ten. He was an opera singer and accompanist at age 12, and at 14 he wrote his first opera. At 18 he had an opera produced in Venice, and at 20 he had another opera produced by LaScala in Milan, the most important opera house in all of Italy. At the age of 22 he had a contract to produce operas for Naples, and there he met his wife-to-be, Isabella Colbron, a Spanish soprano.

Already Rossini was doing new things in opera. He added orchestral accompaniments to the speech-like sung narrative portions called recitatives, where normally there was only a strumming harpsichord.

At 23, Rossini wrote his greatest triumph, *The Barber of Seville*, an opera buffa (comic opera) which is still one of the most popular of Italian operas. The first performance was, however, a disaster, due to a series of stage accidents. The hero, attempting to serenade his girl friend, found the guitar had not been tuned. In tuning it he broke a string, and had to restring it among the mocking laughter of the audience. When Figaro, his assistant, appeared on stage with a guitar, the audience broke up. Each accident added to the funny situation, and finally a cat strolled across the stage ending all hope of a successful performance. Within a week, however, the opera was a hit. Even today the music has become familiar to many young people because of its use with cartoons. Rossini's Overture to his opera *William Tell* was also used as the theme music for the Lone Ranger in the early days of radio.

Now that he was the toast of Italy, Rossini made a triumph tour to Vienna, London (where he was received by King George IV), and finally to Paris (where he was greeted by Napoleon). He settled in Paris where he was acclaimed for his operatic innovations, but after *William Tell* he wrote no more operas. For 39 years he retired from composing, enjoying the good life, good food and witty conversation with his many guests. The reluctant composer could now rest and enjoy life. As a last act he left his large fortune to the Rossini Foundation to care for less fortunate composers.

Suggested Listening: *The Barber of Seville* (*Il Barbiere di Siviglia*)
William Tell Overture

Franz Schubert (1797-1828), the shy son of a rural Viennese school teacher, and a teacher himself, was probably the greatest composer of song who ever lived. He, along with other short-lived composers like Chopin and Mendelssohn, is partly responsible for the idea that nineteenth-century, or "Romantic", composers were remarkable child prodigies who lived exotic lives and died young, burned out at an early age.

Schubert (pronounced shu-bairt) must have shown early talent. His father taught him violin while his brother Ignaz taught him piano. The local choir director also gave him lessons in piano, organ, singing, and music theory. By the time he was eleven years old he had been accepted into the Vienna Imperial Court chapel choir and was being trained for a career in singing at the court school. He played violin in the school orchestra and was occasionally allowed to conduct. There he was taught by the court composer Salieri, who was made famous by his relationship to another great young composer who died early—Mozart. In fact, Salieri's name has often been linked to the possible poisoning of Mozart. At least in Schubert's case, Salieri was very helpful, and continued to teach him for several years. Schubert next attended a training college for teachers and then became a teacher back home at his father's school.

Schubert had to work hard to find time for his real love— composing. By the time he was twenty years old he had already written some very large works, five symphonies and four masses. But he wrote best in small forms, especially the Lied (pronounced leed) or art-song, a form which became newly important in the nineteenth century. Schubert was famous for his beautiful song melodies, and for his exciting and dramatic songs based on great poetry. When he was seventeen he wrote his first great song "Gretchen at the Spinning Wheel" which had a whirring, spinning-wheel-like piano accomlpaniment. When he was eighteen he wrote perhaps his greatest song, the "Erl-King". The "Erl-King" requires the singer to impersonate three people: a father, a sick child, and a ghostly king (death). The father races on horseback carrying his child for help, but the Erl-King, or death, catches up with them at the end of the song. The piano part is almost impossible to play because of the continuous fast repeated chords (horse's hooves) which tire the pianist's hands. This tragic song is a favorite with audiences world-wide.

Schubert managed to write hundreds of songs in his lifetime (as many as 140 in a single year, 1815), including the famous "To Music" and "The Trout". Although he was very shy, he was famous for the "Schubertiads"—evening gatherings of friends where Schubert played the piano and sang his songs. In 1828 he wrote one last set of songs called the "Swan-song". Our expression "swan-song" for someone's last try at something comes from this instance. Sick and very poor, Schubert died in 1828 at the age of 31.

Suggested Listening: "Gretchen at the Spinning Wheel" (*Gretchen am Spinnrade*)
"The Erl-King" (*Erl-Konig*)
"To Music" (*An die Musik*)
"The Trout" (*Die Forelle*)

Robert Schumann, a great German Romantic composer, was born in 1810 in Zwickau, Germany. He came from an intelligent, literary family, but one troubled physically and emotionally. His father was a book seller who encouraged Robert's literary and musical interests, but the father died later of a nervous disease. Robert's sister committed suicide at 19, and two brothers died young. Robert began piano lessons at ten, but his mother was determined that he should be a lawyer, and sent him to Leipzig University. After much persuasion he was allowed to change to music. He began studying piano with Friedrich Wieck, but ruined all chances for a concert career when he crippled his right hand. He had used a mechanical device strapped on his hand to strengthen it. Robert continued to suffer increasing depressions, a mental disorder which gradually overcame him. He began to compose, finding inspiration in the young daughter of his teacher. After a long courtship and court battle with her father, Robert and Clara were married in 1840.

While Clara's concert pianist career blossomed, Robert founded a music newspaper, *Die Neue Zeitschrift für Musik*. In it he wrote essays championing new music. He also wrote a series of famous piano pieces: *Carnival*, featuring a parade of clown-like people, *Papillons* (Butterflies), *Kinderszenen* (Childhood Scenes), and the *Piano Concerto in A minor*. He wrote many beautiful songs (100 in one year—1840), many of them in groups called cycles: *Die Frauenliebe und Leben* (A Woman's Love and Life) and *Dichterliebe* (Poet's Love). During these years the young composer Brahms came to study composition with Robert. Robert's emotional condition worsened and he suffered a nervous breakdown in 1844. Clara increased her concertizing in order to support the large family. In 1854 Robert threw himself in the Rhine River, but was rescued. He was placed in a sanatorium at his own request, and died there two years later. Clara devoted the rest of her life to playing Robert's music, making it known to the world.

Suggested Listening: *Carnival*
Kinderszenen
Dichterliebe

Peter Tchaikovsky (pronounced Chai-kahv-skee), the famous Russian composer of ballet music was born in Votkinsk, Russia (1840-1893). His father was a mining inspector, his mother a cultured French woman, and Peter received a good education from a French governess. When he was ten his family moved to St. Petersburg where he attended a school to prepare him for a law career. His mother died of cholera when he was 14. At 19 he graduated and became a government clerk for a short time, but music kept calling him.

At 21 he entered the St. Petersburg Conservatory to study composition with Anton Rubinstein. He did so well that in 1866 he became professor of harmony at the Moscow Conservatory. Worried about his late start in music, he composed diligently and produced one of his most famous compositions, the Romeo and Juliet Overture in 1869. In 1877 he accepted the bold proposal of marriage from a young conservatory student named Antonina Milyukova, but the marriage ended unhappily and Tchaikovsky attempted to drown himself in the Moscow River. The two never divorced, but lived separately, and she died in an insane asylum in 1917.

Meanwhile, Tchaikovsky had met with good fortune in the guise of a wealthy widowed benefactress, Madame Nadejda von Meck. She had commissioned some works from Tchaikovsky, and offered to support him financially so that he would be free to compose. Strangely enough, they never met, but carried on a long and warm correspondence.

A series of famous compositions featuring beautiful melodies and brilliant orchestration poured from his pen. Ballet music such as Swan Lake, Sleeping Beauty, and Nutcracker Suite have become staples in ballet companies around the world. The Nutcracker, particularly, is performed in most major cities every Christmas. Other dramatic symphonic works were the 1812 Overture, now sometimes performed with real cannon shots, and the fourth, fifth, and sixth (*Pathetique*) Symphonies. He also composed some beautiful lyric songs and operas, and a fine violin concerto.

Although Tchaikovsky's personal life was unhappy, he left a legacy of important ballet and symphonic music.

Suggested Listening: *Romeo and Juliet* Overture
                    Nutcracker Suite
                    1812 Overture

Giuseppe Verdi. If you asked opera-goers to name their favorite opera composer, two names would probably be given: Puccini and Verdi. Americans would probably choose Puccini, but Italians would no doubt pick Verdi. Since his early operas, Verdi's dramatic and tragic music has been loved with a passion by his countrymen.

Verdi was born in 1813 in the tiny Le Roncole, Italy, where his father kept a tavern. Street and tavern singing was part of his early education. The local church organist gave him music lessons, and when he was only eleven, Verdi took over the organist job. His father sent him to Busseto for further training, but Verdi continued to walk the three or four miles home to play for church. When Verdi was 18, Antonio Barezzi, a local merchant, sent him to Milan and paid for his studies. Verdi married Barezzi's daughter Margherita in 1836. By 1840 both his wife and their two small children had died of a fever. Verdi, who had already written several moderately successful operas, became deeply depressed and had to be persuaded to compose again. By 1842 he had another successful opera and his long triumphant career began.

Verdi's early operas had an immediate appeal because of their political undertones. Each opera usually had an aggressive choral march, which could be sung in the political demonstrations. His lyrical melodies began to be played by the street-organs and hummed by the people. After a short successful tour in Paris he returned to Italy and wrote three operas which insured his fame both in and out of Italy. The first, *Rigoletto*, concerning a servant who must sacrifice his daughter to the Duke, contains the famous aria or song "La donna e mobile" (women are fickle). The other two operas depict a gypsy band with its anvil chorus in *Il Trovatore*, and a tragic heroine dying of tuberculosis (a favorite Italian theme) in *La Traviata*. All three are important staples with opera companies today.

Verdi's music became used more and more used to symbolize freedom against oppression for Italy. Verdi's famous opera *Aida*, a "grand" opera complete with a grandiose animal parade, was written for Egypt's Suez Canal opening. He closed his career with two operas which are loved and greatly respected by knowledgeable musicians everywhere. *Falstaff*, a sparkling comedy about a pompous, but life-loving fool, and *Otello*, a deep tragedy concerning the Shakespeare character who wrongly accuses and murders his wife.

When he died in 1901, the "King of Italian Opera" had made arrangements for his fortune to help less fortunate musicians.

Suggested Listening: "La donna e mobile" from *Rigoletto*
                    "Anvil Chorus" from *Il Trovatore*
                    Triumphal March from *Aida*
                    Excerpts from *Falstaff*
                    Excerpts from *Otello*

Richard Wagner (pronounced Ree-kard Vahgner), the great and colorful opera composer was born in Leipzig Germany in 1813, the same year that his father died. He was the youngest of nine children, and so his mother soon married an actor, Ludwig Geyer, to help provide for her familly. But Geyer died when Richard was eight. Wagner's childhood was difficult; he had to move from school to school. He was undisciplined in his school studies and his piano lessons. One day he heard a Beethoven symphony and determined to have a musical career. At 16 he tried studying violin and theory, but gave up both, determining that musical rules were a bother. He began to teach himself, studying Mozart, Haydn, and Beethoven scores, and composing. Interested now, he studied counterpoint and composition seriously with the Cantor (choir director) of the Thomaskirche (St. Thomas Church, where Bach had once been organist). Eventually Wagner had a chance to conduct an orchestra. In 1836 he married an actress—Milnna Planer—but the marriage was never happy. Wagner's wandering continued because he insisted on doing things his way, and had quarrels wherever he went. He was in constant financial trouble, moving to avoid bill collectors.

On a particularly frightening and stormy trip from Russia to Paris, Wagner dreamed up the idea of *The Flying Dutchman* (*Der Fliegende Hollander*) with its graphic storm music. In 1845 he finished *Tannhauser*, and *Lohengrin* in 1848. (The wedding entrance used by most brides today comes from *Lohengrin*.) During this period he wrote a series of essays expounding some new ideas about art. He devleoped his idea of *Gesamtkunstwerk* (a total art work) which would be a perfect blend of music, story, scenery and costumes: the music-drama.

He began to compose both the text and music for a huge four-day opera cycle, *Der Ring des Nibelungen*, complete with a magic gold ring, dwarfs, gods and flying horses. Also written during this time was *Tristan und Isolde*, a great love story. It was a very important musical influence on later composers because of its new wandering harmonies and endless melody. Other famous operas followed: *Parsifal* and *Die Meistersinger* (The Master Signer). In spite of the important operas he was writing, Wagner continued to alienate people, and no one would produce the operas. But his fortune changed dramatically in 1864 when King Ludwig II, the "mad" king of Bavaria, became his benefactor. Cosima Liszt left her husband Hans von Bulow for Wagner during this time, and they married in 1870. Now with the aid of Ludwig, a huge center was built at Bayreuth for performing Wagner's operas. Wagner had lived long enough to see his dreams coming true. He died in 1883.

For a time Wagner's music was used by Hitler's Nazis as political music, and after World War II it was banned in some countries. It took some time for his music to be returned to its proper place. Once again Wagner's operas are performed annually at Bayreuth, now under the direction of his grandson.

Wagner revolutionized opera with his music-dramas. He created new musical instruments, began a new school of dramatic singing, a new conducting style, and above all, a new direction for harmony. The direction of nineteenth-century music was changed because of this one man.

Suggested Listening: *The Flying Dutchman* Overture (*Der Fliegende Hollander*)
                    The Wedding March from *Lohengrin*
                    Overture to *Die Meistersinger*

THE TWENTIETH CENTURY

THE TWENTIETH CENTURY

Major Historical Events

1900	Boxer Rebellion
1903	Wright brothers' first airplane flight
1905	Freud founds analysis
1906	San Francisco earthquake
1908	Model T Ford first produced
1910	Discovery of protons and electrons
1912	Titanic sinks
1914	World War I begins
1917	Russian Revolution
1918	World War I ends
1920	First commercial radio broadcast
1924	Stalin comes to power in Russia
1927	Lindbergh's solo flight across the Atlantic
1929	New York stock market crash
1930	Penicillin discovered
1932	Franklin Roosevelt elected president
1933	Hitler becomes Chancellor of Germany
1936	Spanish Civil War
1939	Hitler invades Poland
1941	Pearl Harbor attacked, U.S. enters World War II
1945	First atom bomb dropped
1945	World War II ends
1950	Korean War begins
1951	NATO formed
1957	First satellite launched
1961	First man in space
1963	President Kennedy assassinated
1968	Martin Luther King assassinated
1969	First men on the moon
1974	Nixon resigns as President after Watergate
1975	Vietnam War ends
1979	Iranian Hostage Crisis
1980	Ronald Reagan elected president

Music

1900	Puccini - *Tosca*
1905	Debussy - *La Mer*
1909	Schoenberg - *Piano Pieces, Op. 11*
1910	Vaughan Williams - *Sea Symphony*
1913	Stravinsky - *Rite of Spring*

1915	Ives - *Concord Sonata*
1917	Respighi - *Fountains of Rome*
1918	Prokofiev - *Classical Symphony*
1920	Holst - *The Planets*
1924	Gershwin - *Rhapsody in Blue*
1925	Berg - *Wozzeck*
1927	Stravinsky - *Oedipus Rex*
1927	Kern - *Show Boat*
1928	Weill - *The Threepenny Opera*
1930	Stravinsky - *Symphony of Psalms*
1934	Thomson - *Four Saints in Three Acts*
1935	Gershwin - *Porgy and Bess*
1937	Orff - *Carmina Burana*
1937	Shostakovich - *Fifth Symphony*
1942	Rodgers and Hammerstein - *Oklahoma!*
1944	Copland - *Appalachian Spring*
1944	Bartok - *Concerto for Orchestra*
1945	Britten - *Peter Grimes*
1947	Prokofiev - *War and Peace*
1949	Barber - *Knoxville: Summer of 1915*
1951	Menotti - *Amahl and the Night Visitors*
1951	Boulez - *Polyphonie X*
1956	Lerner and Loewe - *My Fair Lady*
1956	Bernstein and Sondheim - *West Side Story*
1957	Poulenc - *Dialogues of the Carmelites*
1962	Britten - *War Requiem*
1964	The Beatles arrive in U.S.
1969	Woodstock Rock Festival

Visual Arts

1902	Monet - *Waterloo Bridge*
1906	Derain - *London Bridge*
1909	Frank Lloyd Wright - Robie House, Chicago
1921	Picasso - *Three Musicians*
1923	Klee - *At the Mountain of the Bull*
1930	Wood - *American Gothic*
1930	Hopper - *Early Sunday Morning*
1937	Picasso - *Guernica*
1943	Chagall - *Crucifixion*

Major Artists of the period:

Spanish: Picasso, Gris, Dali

American: Wood, Wright Hopper, O'Keefe, Rockwell, Close, Pollock, Segal, Kandinsky, Wyeth, Lichtenstein, Warhol

French: Cezanne, Monet, Derain, Chagall, Braque, Miro, Matisse

British: Hockney, Moore

Swiss: Klee

Literature

1901	Shaw - *Caesar and Cleopatra*
1904	Chekav - *The Cherry Orchard*
1904	Barrie - *Peter Pan*
1911	Wharton - *Ethan Frome*
1913	Lawrence - *Sons and Lovers*
1913	Mann - *Death in Venice*
1913	Proust - *Remembrance of Things Past*
1917	Yeats - *Wild Swans at Coole*
1918	Cather - *My Antonia*
1920	Lewis - *Main Street*
1922	Eliot - *The Waste Land*
1922	Joyce - *Ullyses*
1924	Shaw - *St. Joan*
1925	Fitzgerald - *The Great Gatsby*
1926	Hemingway - *The Sun Also Rises*
1927	Woolf - *To the Lighthouse*
1929	Wolfe - *Look Homeward, Angel*
1931	O'Neill - *Morning Becomes Elektra*
1936	Dos Passos - *U.S.A.*
1938	Wilder - *Our Town*
1939	Steinbeck - *The Grapes of Wrath*
1939	Joyce - *Finnegan's Wake*
1940	Hemingway - *For Whom the Bell Tolls*
1943	Sartre - *Being and Nothingness*
1947	Williams - *A Streetcar Named Desire*
1949	Orwell - *1984*
1949	Miller - *Death of a Salesman*
1950	Eliot - *The Cocktail Party*
1954	Thomas - *Under Milk Wood*
1955	Faulkner - *A Fable*
1957	Kerouac - *On the Road*
1958	Agee - *A Death in the Family*
1960	Drury - *Advise and Consent*
1962	Albee - *Who's Afraid of Virginia Woolf?*
1966	Porter - *Collected Stories of Katherine Anne Porter*
1968	Roth - *Goodbye Columbus*
1972	Wright - *Collected Poems*
1976	Bellow - *Humboldt's Gift*
1979	Cheever - *The Stories of John Cheever*
1980	Mailer - *The Executioner's Song*
1982	Updike - *Rabbit is Rich*

Major Writers of The Period:

American: Lewis, Dreiser, Stein, Cummings, Hemingway, Fitzgerald, Faulkner, Wilder, Mailer, O'Neill, Steinbeck, Bellow, Cheever, Updike, Michener

French: Proust, Bergson, Beckett, Sartre, Camus

British: Joyce, Shaw, Eliot, Kipling, Waugh, Russell, Woolf, Yeats, Lawrence

Russian: Solzhenitsyn, Sholokhov, Pasternak

Other Nationalities: Neruda, Mann, Hesse

Film

1915	*Birth of a Nation*
1929	*The Jazz Singer*
1930	*All Quiet on the Western Front*
1934	*It Happened One Night*
1939	*Gone With the Wind*
1939	*The Wizard of Oz*
1940	*The Grapes of Wrath*
1943	*Casablanca*
1946	*The Best Years of Our Lives*
1948	*Hamlet*
1950	*Singing in the Rain*
1951	*A Streetcar Named Desire*
1954	*On the Waterfront*
1957	*The Bridge on the River Kwai*
1959	*Ben-Hur*
1961	*West Side Story*
1962	*Lawrence of Arabia*
1964	*My Fair Lady*
1965	*The Sound of Music*
1967	*Guess Who's Coming to Dinner?*
1968	*Funny Girl*
1970	*Patton*
1972	*The Godfather*
1973	*The Sting*
1975	*One Flew Over the Cuckoo's Nest*
1976	*Rocky*
1977	*Annie Hall*
1978	*The Deer Hunter*
1979	*Kramer vs. Kramer*
1980	*Ordinary People*
1981	*Chariots of Fire*
1982	*Ghandi*
1982	*E. T., The Extra-Terrestrial*
1984	*Amadeus*
1985	*Out of Africa*

The best word to describe music of the 20th century is eclectic. Styles of music have taken many directions which have continually provided listeners with a wide array of music from which to choose. Even within any particular style there is enormous variety. In the broad view, all of this diverse, individualistic activity is a natural consequence of the individualism begun in the 19th century. But there have been other influences that have shaped and defined the music of this century.

It was at the beginning of the 20th century that our modern popular, mass culture was defined, and technology had a great deal to do with the changing tastes. From the first decade of this century, motion pictures quickly grew to be enormously popular. And, of course, music was part of this popularity. In the silent movie days the film would always be accompanied by continuous music. With the introduction of sound, music played a more intricate role, whether the picture was a musical featuring many songs and dance

154

numbers, or if music was used as an added background to help communicate the story and mood of a spoken drama.

The phonograph made music readily available whenever the listener wanted to hear it. Now for the first time you didn't need an orchestra to hear a symphony, you only needed a phonograph and a recording of an orchestra playing a symphony.

Radio, too, made music readily accessible to millions of people all over the world. The new invention quickly catipulted to world wide popularity in the 1920's, and today most people still listen to the radio. With the flick of a dial you can hear music of almost any variety, changing the station as often as you wish, according to your tastes. This altered life greatly, and not only musically. Radio unified the world. All over the planet people could tune in to hear the same events reported as they happened. And music had an immediate audience of hundreds of millions of people.

Later, around 1950, television was added to the available mass media. Like radio, television can broadcast music to millions instantly with the added bonus that we can not only hear the music, but also see the performers.

All in all, the electronic age has entirely changed our relationship with music. It is always available, on film, on radio, on television, or on record. We hear music nearly everywhere we go, in supermarkets, at doctors' offices, in airports, elevators, shopping malls, restaurants, etc. This constant availability can't help but change not only the music, but our tastes as well. In these contexts it is imperative that the ever present music be quickly accessible, short and relatively light and consumable. We simply couldn't digest a long complex symphony every time we turn on the radio, television, or phonograph. Ironically, the overabundance of music in modern culture puts limits on both the music and the listener.

Art Music in the 20th Century

A certain stream of composers and performers have continued to approach music in the tradition of concert music of the previous centuries. Symphonies are still composed, and operas are still written, along with chamber music, piano music and choral music. In short, nearly every type of piece begun since the Baroque has continued in some way or another, however changed they may seem to be from earlier counterparts.

Composers working in this tradition have gone in many varying directions. One main stream was simply to continue the Romantic approach to music from the 19th century. Although the harmony often became more dissonant, a great deal of serious music written before World War II was a continuation of Romanticism. But along with this extended tradition there was a great deal of experimenting. Some composers in this century have been most interested in creating new harmonic vocabularies, resulting in a breakdown of the tonal tradition of music. Melody, orchestration, texture and rhythm were continually redefined by these experimenters. In a reaction to 19th century Romanticism, some composers strove for a more objective style, one free of emotion, stressing simply music for music's sake. This parallels the similar aims of abstract visual art in this same era. After the second world war this trend toward objectivity was well in place. Certainly there were still lush, Romantic pieces being written by some, but the general trend in aesthetics had swung away from this toward abstraction. This could sometimes be referred to as an 'academic' style of music, for it was, for the most part centered in university music communities.

In more recent years, since the late 1970's, there seems to be a trend toward more accessible, less abstract music among serious composers. One important movement of the 1970's was what some call "minimalism". Musically, this trend was to move to an extremely simple harmonic and melodic vocabulary, using repetition as a unifying and driving force in the form of a piece.

Art Music Composers in the 20th Century

Economically, the serious arts have changed drastically in his century as compared to earlier times. In early Christian and Medieval times, it was the Church that was the chief musical center and benefactor of composers and musicians. In the Renaissance and the Baroque, the Church and the royal court were both centers of musical activities, and composers sought court or church appointments as a means of making a living. In the 18th century the court virtually took over this role, as the church became less of the controlling force and center of Western society. During the 19th century, the new middle class was the main consumer of music, as the artistocracy played less and less of a role. The composer/performer's main income was actually provided by the sale of concert tickets and published music. In the 20th century, serious music has centered itself in two closely related, but different environments: 1) the non-profit arts organization, and 2) colleges and universities. Non-profit music organizations are designed to continue to make available art forms that can no longer pay for themselves, simply because economics have changed. All symphony orchestras and opera companies in this country fall into this category, along with many smaller and varied musical organizations. These do have income from ticket sales, but it is not enough to pay for all costs. A large profitable symphony of the 19th century becomes unprofitable in the 20th century because of musicians' salaries, conductor fees, concert hall maintenance fees, etc. But people still love this music and want to hear it performed. Wealthy patrons of the arts make contributions, as do large corporations, to these groups to insure their continued existence. Grants are also available from the government for these organizations. Most of these non-profit organizations have been primarily committed to presenting the great music of the past, not the music of the present century. It is difficult to explain why this is so. Perhaps it is because people love the familiar pieces, and are suspect of new ones. Perhaps they haven't had the chance, for whatever reason, to hear enough of a variety of 20th century serious music to acquire the taste for it. Perhaps the concert going public simply prefers old music to new music. Whatever the reason, serious composers in this century have had limited success with commissions from large non-profit organizations. There are certainly exceptions, composers who have been able to make a successful living writing music in this arena, but it has not been fruitful for the majority of composers.

Universities and colleges, then, have become the centers of serious musical composition in our century. Composers can have academic careers, teaching courses or lessons in music, and have time to compose as well. The university environment can provide performers and ensembles for performance of new pieces.

The music of the 20th century has, in less than a 100 years, gone through violent changes in attitudes and expression that make the previous musical revolutions seem minor. The search for individuality by each composer and for a new and different form of expression has led to a variety of compositional techniques that are basically experimental in nature. Composers of the 20th century felt that the basic ingredients of all music—pitch, melody, harmony, rhythm, and tone color had been explored and defined to their maximum by previous composers, and that it was time to find new means of expression. The following is a brief citing of some of the more common compositional elements of the 20th century.

Pitch

The basic 12 tones of the octave have been divided into quarter tones (24 pitches to the octave), and eighth tones (48 different pitches to the octave). This device is called micro-tonality and requires a new form of notation and very exceptional performers in order to be realized.

Melody

Generally speaking, the melodies of 20th century composers exhibit a more angular contour than those of their predecessors. The melodic line is rhythmically more complex and employs the use of wide intervals; in addition, it frequently encompasses the extreme range of the voice or instrument. Composers use non-traditional scale patterns or use a mixture of two different modes.

Harmony

Twentieth-century harmony is more freely dissonant but tends to move to consonant harmonies at cadences. Some composers have achieved dissonance through the practice of bitonality or polytonality (the use of two or more key centers at the same time). Twentieth-century music is exciting because it is so often unexpected. The listener is unable to predict the direction of the harmony.

Rhythm

Generally, the rhythm of 20th century music is more complex than that of its predecessors. Rhythmic irregularity and variety are achieved through the use of constantly changing meters or by the alternation of compound and simple meters. Twentieth-century composers make much use of meters that are of odd-numbered metric patterns (5/4, 7/8, 11/8, etc.).

Expressive Markings

Composers of the 20th century are usually very specific in their requirements for performance. A metronomic marking is usually indicated, and the individual parts are very precisely marked with appropriate expressive markings. The traditional Italian terms are frequently written in the composer's native language. There is great freedom on the part of the composer to communicate directly with the performer.

Popular Music of the 20th Century

The rise of mass culture, or popular culture, began to be a strong presence at the beginning of the century. As previously mentioned, technology played a role in this development. But since technology itself is basically neutral (after all, any style of music can be broadcast on the radio), there must have been some major trends in public tastes and musical fashions that alligned to create popular culture as it has been defined. The following is a brief look at musical trends and styles rooted in the popular, rather than serious, music line of development:

1. **Ragtime.** This was an early style of jazz, very rhythmic and syncopated, that had its beginnings in the Mississippi River region in the late 19th century. Chicago was its later center of activity. Scott Joplin is certainly the best known composer of this style.

2. **The Musical Stage.** The "classic" period of the American popular song, roughly 1925-1950, was centered largely around the Broadway and Hollywood musicals. All of the great songwriters of the period—George Gershwin, Jerome Kern, Cole Porter, Irving Berlin, Richard Rodgers — concentrated their efforts in these two centers of activity, producing what are today called "standards". Of course, the Broadway and Hollywood musical continues to thrive, but the rock era has changed the picture. "Standards" from the Broadway stage or Silver Screen are a rarer and rarer phenomenon after 1950. However, there is still considerable activity, particularly in the field of musical theatre. Important composers of this genre since 1950 are Frank Loesser, Jerry Herman, Marvin Hamlisch, and Stephen Sandheim.

3. **Blues.** This style came from the south, probably again in the Mississippi River basin. Its beginnings were in the black culture, and the subject matter is generally of suffering of some kind. Harmonies are extremely simple, the emphasis being on the performer's improvisation. Blues is a style of music defined by the performer, not the composer.

4. **Jazz.** The ingredients that culminated in jazz are varied, but most came from black musical roots. Ragtime, the Negro spiritual, and Blues all certainly played a role. As jazz evolved, there were many different trends and varieties, but all of them were defined by the improvisation of performers. Jazz musicians, such as Charlie Parker or Ella Fitzgerald, have been some of the best virtuosos of the century in terms of improvisational imagination and technical skill. For the most part, though not always, jazz has been a rather objective art form. There has often been a detached, abstract quality to jazz styles, clearly separating it from the strong emotion of the Blues, or for that matter, from the subjective approach of the Romantic tradition.

5. **Rock.** Rock, or Rock 'n Roll, began as a style in the 1950's. Early Rock 'n Roll was harmonically simple, usually relying on just a few chords, but derived its energy from a strong, steady rhythmic drive. At its beginning it was primarily music for the young, mainly being dance music. The wide influence of The Beatles in the 1960's produced a rapid change in rock styles, and songs became more harmonically and lyrically complex without losing the basic appeal of the rock style. It has been the most commercially successsful style of music in history, creating incalculable amounts of money from radio play, record sales, and concerts. Rock music is as diverse and varied as the other styles of the 20th century, providing contrasts such as the "soul" variety, "heavy-metal", "new wave", "rockabilly", or simply the latest rock ballad.

6. **Country.** This style grew out of the folk songs native to the American South and West, but in its full bloom became as diverse as other styles. Early on Nashville became the center for its activity and remains so today. Although difficult to define, country music is easily recognizable upon listening, often characterized by simple lyrics that tell a story.

In addition to these styles there has been a growing serious interest in folk music of all varieties from all world cultures. American folk music has generally told a story, a ballad, or has been in some way politically motivated. Folk styles around the world vary greatly, sometimes closely tied to folk instruments that are foreign to our western culture.

The Musical Present

In summary, all the styles discussed previously are alive and well in some form or another today. Musical variety is extreme in contrasts and in personal tastes. But perhaps the most fascinating phenomenon to observe is how all these diverse styles borrow from and influence one another. Most of us tend to think of styles as being compartmentalized, each one following its own exclusive course. The reality is probably that they are all intricately inter-related.

If we are perceptive listeners we can broaden our tastes and our imaginations by being open and aware of the different styles of music that are present in our world. If we only focus our interest on those styles we know that we are sure to like, without ever venturing further, then we are certainly cutting ourselves off from the possibility of the excitement and reward of discovery.

Important Composers of the 20th Century

The Beatles. Probably no other group was more popular, or has had more influence on the popular music scene than the Beatles. The group consisted originally of John Lennon (born in Liverpool, as were all the Beatles, on October 9, 1940), Paul McCartney (born June 18, 1942) and George Harrison (born February 25, 1943). From 1955 to 1960 there were several name changes, from the Quarrymen to the Silver Beatles, and changes also in personnel. By 1958, Lennon, McCartney, and Harrison were together, and in 1960 they were joined by Peter Best on drums, Stu Sutcliffe on guitar and singer Tony

158

Sheridan. In 1960 the group worked and recorded in Hamburg, Germany. In 1961, when the Silver Beatles returned to London, they were discovered by Brian Epstein, their future manager, at a Liverpool dive, the Cavern Club. Ringo Starr (born Richard Starkey in Liverpool on July 17, 1940) joined the group in 1962, replacing Peter Best on drums.

Now known as the Beatles, the group of four released their first hit single in England, "Love Me Do". John Lennon played, as needed, rhythm guitar, harmonica, piano, and sang vocals. Paul McCartney played bass, piano, banjo, trumpet, and also did vocals. George Harrison was on lead guitar, sitar, piano, and vocals, and Ringo Starr was drummer, assisting on vocals. In 1964 the Beatles hit the United States with two singles, "I Want To Hold Your Hand" and "I Saw Her Standing There". Their tour of the U.S. in the same year started the Beatle craze, Beatlemania, which has lasted to this day. Young "groupies" followed them on their travels; groups both in England and the U.S. imitated their hair and dress styles. Movies such as "A Hard Day's Night", "Magical Mystery Tour", the animated psychedelic film "Yellow Submarine" and "Let It Be" were made from 1964 to 1970, and increased their popularity as youth idols.

But rather than a short-lived popularity, the Beatle's influence grew because of their varied creativity. Constantly trying new ideas, their songs ranged from the simpler hit single songs of the mid 60's such as "She Loves You", "A Hard Day's Night" and "Ticket to Ride", to more sophisticated and serious songs like the sad "Eleanor Rigby" and "In My Life". During this time John was writing and publishing books, all were collaborating on films, George was writing songs, and John and Paul were stretching the limits, and the mind, with "Lucy in the Sky With Diamonds", "Strawberry Fields Forever", and "I Am the Walrus". Increasingly the group tried new studio recording techniques, electronic devices, and new instruments (the sitar, and a complete classical string orchestra). John and Ringo began acting in films.

In 1968 the group formed their own record company, Apple, and issued such favorites as "Hey Jude". But trouble was brewing. The group had grown long hair, a real change from their short, carefully groomed hair of the early sixties. Instead of their uniform neat dress suits, they now wore individual outfits influenced by their exploration of Eastern mysticism, meditation, drugs, and the influence of an Indian guru. By 1969 the rift in the group was wide, and each had separate interests. John Lennon had married Yoko Ono and pursued more Oriental experimentation. Paul McCartney had married Linda Eastman (forming the group Wings), and secluded himself in the English country-side, writing more old-fashioned songs. In 1974 the Beatles partnership legally ended, though rumors of a reunion persisted until John was tragically murdered outside his New York apartment in 1980. In 1981 the remaining three recorded a tribute to John written by George Harrison, "All Those Years Ago".

The Beatles will long be remembered for their creativity, for the great variety of musical styles, use of new harmonies, new instrumental sounds, and multi-media productions. Their influence on already two generations of youth has been immense.

Suggested Listening: "I Want to Hold Your Hand"
"Eleanor Rigby"
"Lucy In the Sky With Diamonds"
"Strawberry Fields Forever"
"Hey Jude"

Leonard Bernstein. Few men in history have had as many varied talents as Bernstein. He has had an important career as a symphony conductor, composer of classical music, composer of Broadway musicals, and university lecturer and poet.

He was born in 1918 in Lawrence, Massachusetts to Russian-Jewish parents. From 1935 to 1939 he attended Harvard University and studied counterpoint and fugue with

159

Walter Piston, the famous writer of music theory textbooks. After graduation he attended Curtis Institute in Philadelphia and studied orchestration with the choral composer Randall Thompson. Summers were spent at Tanglewood studying conducting with Koussevitzky.

Bernstein became assistant conductor of the New York Philharmonic, the finest orchestra in the U.S. in 1943. His big break came when he stepped in at the last minute to substitute for conductor Bruno Walter in a very difficult program. He became principal conductor of the New York Philharmonic in 1958, the first American-born conductor the orchestra ever had. (The great Arturo Toscanini had earlier built the reputation of the orchestra, causing an increasing demand for Europeans as conductors. Young Americans seldom had a chance to conduct in their homeland.) During the time Bernstein conducted the New York Philharmonic, from 1958-69, he televised a series of Young People's Concerts. These programs featured young teenagers and children as concert performers with the orchestra. The programs were very popular with families throughout the U.S. because Bernstein talked about music on the programs and made it easily understood. These programs were also recorded and the records became best-sellers in record stores. With these concert series, Bernstein began a lifetime of introducing audiences to classical music. Bernstein's programs were also enhanced by his own talent as a pianist. He often played the solo in a piano concerto while conducting the orchestra from the keyboard.

Equally important were his Broadway musicals. In 1957 he composed *West Side Story* for Broadway (which also became a movie), a modern New York ghetto version of the Romeo and Juliet story. He also wrote *Candide* (the music has been used for commercials), a wonderful musical travelog based on Moliere's story. Other works were *Wonderful Town*, about New York, a ballet, *Fancy Free*, the impressive *Chichester Psalms* for choir and orchestra, and the film music for *On the Waterfront*, starring Marlon Brando. The stage show Mass was written in response to a request by Jackie Kennedy, widow of the assassinated President, for the opening of the Kennedy Center in Washington, D.C. in 1971. It features a guitar-player hero/priest.

Bernstein's exciting and dramatic music features complex, jazz and Latin American rhythms, and pictures the variety of ethnic America. For thirty years he has used his rare ability to bring both understanding and the joy of music to the world.

Suggested Listening: *West Side Story*
Candide
Chichester Psalms
Mass

Benjamin Britten (1913-1976) is one of the most popular twentieth-century English composers. He was born on St. Cecilia Day (the patron saint of musicians). He grew up in wealthy surroundings; his father was an orthodontist, his mother an amateur singer. Britten himself showed great talent early, playing the piano and improvising. He studied piano, viola and composition at 13. By the time he was 16 he had written numerous works, including a symphony, six quartets, and ten piano sonatas. At 17 he entered the Royal College of Music. He progressed rapidly in composition but found the atmosphere stifling, and after four years of study he left to take a job doing film scoring. During this job which lasted four years, he learned to compose rapidly and with economy.

After a short period in the U.S., he returned to England, and was a conscientious objector during World War II. After the war (1948) he helped found the Aldeburgh Festival, devoted to performing short operas by English composers. He learned to economize in order to have his works performed, scoring works for an orchestra reduced to 12 (as in the *Turn of the Screw*).

Britten was particularly successful in composing modern "parables" for church performance (such as *Curlew River, The Burning Fiery Furnace,* and *The Prodigal Son*) which involved the whole congregation. His version of a medieval miracle play, *Noye's Fludde,* engulfs the audience in the rising flood, and they must sing a hymn for help. *Let's Make An Opera* also involves audience participation. *The Young Person's Guide to the Orchestra* has become a standard listening tool in elementary schools.

Britten's varied, educational, yet moving and dramatic music has enriched not only English life, but the life of children, youth, and adults around the world.

Suggested Listening: *Noye's Fludde*
The Young Person's Guide to the Orchestra
A Ceremony of Carols
Rejoice in the Lamb

Aaron Copland. Probably the most "American" of living composers, Copland has long been respected and honored for his contributions toward an "American" style of music.

Like Gershwin, he, too, was born in Brooklyn (in 1900) to Russian-Jewish immigrants. He began music lessons later than usual, piano at 13, and theory at 17, with Rubin Goldmark (also Gershwin's teacher). Copland's turning point came with the decision to go to France to continue serious study at Fontainebleau. In 1921 he began private composition lessons with Nadia Boulanger and was to become her most famous pupil. She encouraged him to cultivate an American music rather than imitating the French conservatory style. (His orchestra piece *El Salon Mexico* was an attempt at an American sound with Mexican popular themes.)

He returned to New York in 1924 without a means of support, but two early published piano pieces, *The Cat and The Mouse* and *Passacaglia,* soon brought him recognition. The important conductor Koussevitzky took him under his wing, and in 1927, Copland performed his own Concerto for piano and orchestra under Koussevitzky's baton. The immediate popularity of the jazzy concerto launched his career. (It is interesting to note another parallel with Gershwin's life. Gershwin's first great success had occurred three years before with the jazz symphonic work *Rhapsody in Blue.*) Copland often used jazz or other syncopated (off-beat) rhythmic elements in his music.

Copland began to try other vehicles for composition. He wrote radio and film scores, including music for *The City, Of Mice and Men,* and *Our Town.* Later (1950), he won an Oscar for the film score to *The Heiress.* He also wrote a large amount of vocal music, and chamber music.

Perhaps Copland's most important and successful venture was his work with ballet. His scores for *Billy the Kid* (1938), *Rodeo* (1942), and *Appalachian Spring* (1944) were not only important musically for their folk style, they also provided impetus for Martha Graham, the choreographer, to establish an American style of ballet. *Appalachian Spring* received the Pulitzer Prize in 1945.

Copland's *Lincoln Portrait* for narrator and orchestra (1942) was another greatly popular work. Such famous people as Adlai Stevenson, Eleanor Roosevelt, and Marian Anderson performed the narration with major orchestras.

Copland has also had a highly successful career as a composition teacher at Tanglewood, as a lecturer at Harvard, among other places, and as a writer of books. He has been extensively honored with prizes, and received honorary doctorates from such distinguished universities as Princeton, Harvard, Rutgers, Brandeis, New York University, and Columbia. He also continues to tour as a guest conductor. Certainly he still deserves the title of "Dean of American Composers".

Suggested Listening: *El Salon Mexico*
Appalachian Spring
Lincoln Portrait

Claude Debussy. This great musical Impressionist was born in France in 1862. His father planned a navy career for him, but a pupil of Chopin recognized his talent and prepared him for the Paris Conservatory which he entered at age ten. He did not win all the prizes at the Conservatory but he acquired a good background. When he was recommended to Madame von Meck (Tchaikovsky's patron) as a piano teacher for her children, he took the job and had a chance to travel to Switzerland, Italy, and Russia. He became acquainted with the music the great Russian composers, Borodin, Mussorgsky, and of course, Tchaikovsky.

Back at the conservatory, he graduated in 1884, and won the Prix de Rome, a prize which paid expenses to study and compose in Rome. He wrote several choral works and cantatas, and returned to Paris.

He now became acquainted with some French Symbolist poets, particularly Mallarme, and discovered a love for oriental music at the Paris Exhibition of 1889. His music began to reflect these interests and an emphasis on mood, color, and atmosphere. His famous piano compositions include: *Petite suite, Suite bergamasque* (includes the famous "Clair de lune"), *Children's Corner* (written for his daughter "Chou-Chou"), 12 Preludes, *Estampes,* and *Images.*

Debussy wrote a number of choral compositions and used a wordless women's choir in the three Nocturnes for orchestra. Other well-known orchestral works are: *Prelude à l'après-midi d'un faune* (Prelude to the Afternoon of a Faun, the hallmark of Impressionism) and *La Mer* (the Sea).

Also important are his ballet, *Jeux,* his opera *Pelleas and Mélisande*, and some lovely solo songs. He died a slow, painful death from brain cancer in 1918.

Debussy is regarded as the founder of musical Impressionism, using delicate musical colors in the way French Impressionist painters did. To achieve these effects, he used exotic scales, pentatonic (5-tone) and whole-tone. He used series of dischords and oriental sounding perfect fifths, and "painted" it all with a lovely orchestral palette.

Suggested Listening: *Children's Corner*
*Nocturnes (*particularly "Sirenes")
Prelude à l'après-midi d'un faune
(Prelude to the Afternoon of a Faun)
La Mer

Duke Ellington. Edward Kennedy Ellington, known as "Duke", was one of the most important black jazz musicians. He was born in Washington, D. C. in 1899, the son of a butler, and the grandson of a policeman. Duke came from a religious family and even went to church twice on Sundays, first to his mother's Baptist church, and then to his father's African Methodist Episcopal church. He later prided himself on having read the Bible completely four times. He took his first serious piano lessons from a Miss Clinkscales (her real name) when he was seven, but often skipped to play baseball. Later he had jobs in the ballpark as a vendor, and later as a dishwasher. Duke loved to play ragtime piano and wrote "Soda Fountain Rag" in 1914. During these early year he worked with various jazz bands.

In 1923 he went to New York and organized his own "big band". Starting with ten players, the band grew under his leadership for the next 50 years. He revolutionized jazz with his big band sound and complex arrangements. Ellington's players were required to be both good improvisers and fine music readers. Duke composed jazz pieces with his particular band sound in mind. His pieces were also influenced by classical music, and Debussy and Delius are the influential composers most often mentioned.

The band began to tour all over Europe. Duke, too, received honors, particularly honorary doctorates from Yale (1967) and Columbia (1973). In 1965 he gave a sacred concert at Grace Cathedral in San Francisco, and a second one in 1968 at St. John the Divine Cathedral in New York City. In 1969 he was given a birthday party at the White House and presented with the Medal of Freedom by President Nixon. After Duke's death in 1974, his son Mercer took over his band.

Suggested Listening: "Mood Indigo"
"Satin Doll"

George Gershwin was one of the first composers to bridge the gap between popular music and classical music. By using jazz elements in classical music he started a trend that spread to Europe and continues today.

George (really Jacob Gershvin) was born in Brooklyn in 1898, the son of a Russian immigrant. He and his brother Ira (who would later become a famous lyricist—writer of words—to George's tunes) grew up in the crowded streets of New York's East Side. They both took sporadic piano lessons with a local piano teacher. At sixteen George got a job in Tin Pan Alley at Remick's, a music publishing house. He played popular song hits on the piano, the way customers were urged to buy the sheet music. Seeing an easy opportunity to make money, he began writing and playing his own songs for customers. Such hits as "Swanee" (written when he was 19 and sung by Al Jolson), "Fascinatin' Rhythm", "Lady Be Good", and "The Man I Love" were a result of his "education" in Tin Pan Alley. He began writing musical comedies for Broadway, which showcased his and Ira's songs.

An important turning point in his career occurred when he met Paul Whiteman, a classical cellist and orchestra conductor who was interested in jazz. He encouraged the self-conscious Gershwin to try his hand at using jazz in a serious symphonic work. The result, *Rhapsody in Blue,* for piano and orchestra, was performed in 1924 to great acclaim. Fearful because of his lack of classical training, Gershwin had hidden the score until the last minute, and then arrived late at the concert, afraid of laughter and derision. Almost overnight he received a good income from performances, records, and sheet music sales of Rhapsody in Blue. More importantly he had dignified jazz, bringing it in from the alleyways to the concert hall. Composers now had a new, lively musical tool for compostion.

Other recognition soon followed. His musical comedy, *Of Thee I Sing*, won a Pulitzer Prize. His artistic stature rose with the composition of other serious classical works such as the *Concerto in F* for piano and orchestra, the symphonic poem *American in Paris* (later made into a movie with Gene Kelly), and especially his opera about life in the black ghettos of South Carolina, *Porgy and Bess. Porgy and Bess* contained such popular songs as "Summertime", "I Got Plenty O' Nothin'", "It Ain't Necessarily So", and "Bess You Is My Woman Now". It continues to receive international acclaim and was the first American opera performed in Russia.

Self-conscious about his spotty education, Gershwin tried throughout his life to take composition lessons from famous acquaintances, but many refused, saying that he was already successful. Gershwin died tragically, at the height of his career, from a brain tumor. He was 39.

Suggested Listening: *Rhapsody in Blue*
Porgy and Bess

Philip Glass. The new contemporary avant-garde group of composers called "Minimalists" has often been criticized for writing minimal music with minimal talent and with minimal influence on history. But Philip Glass is proving the critics wrong. His continuing popular successes with operatic premieres in such centers as Paris, New York, and Stuttgart prove that the movement is not short lived.

Although minimalists make use of long, hypnotic musical repetitions, Glass's life has been anything but dull and repetitious. He was born in Baltimore in 1937, and was the grandson of Russian-Jewish immigrants. He worked in his father's record store as a teenager while studying flute at the Peabody Conservatory. When he was fifteen he entered the University of Chicago to study piano, and, while there, wrestled in the featherweight category. In 1962 he completed a Master's degree at Juilliard in New York City, where he studied composition with Persichetti.

In 1964 he began a series of important foreign travels. A Fullbright grant enabled him to study the discipline of musical counterpoint with Nadia Boulanger, the great teacher of many famous musicians such as Aaron Copland. Also extremely important to his career was his introduction to Hindu ragas by the great Indian sitar performer Ravi Shankar. He wandered to Morocco to study complex repeating North African rhythms. He married JoAnne Akalaitis, one of a traveling group of actors, and together they traveled to the Himalayas.

He returned to New York and began using the techniques and musical tools he had observed. Repeating a musical idea over and over, Glass gradually added small, minimal changes to the music, which results in an almost hypnotizing sound. The origins of this kind of music lie in Indian music, like the performance of a sitar player. Two pieces resulted: "Strung Out" (1967) for electric violin and "600 Lines" written for his own performing ensemble, the Glass Ensemble, an amplified ensemble of keyboard instruments, winds, and voice.

In 1975 he collaborated with Robert Wilson on an opera, *Einstein on the Beach.* A "dream play" which moves slowly and almost motionless for five hours, it explores the Einstein theory of the relativity of space by saying that the experience is relative to each listener. He uses the recurring images of a train and space ship, and in the same way repeats small rhythmic patterns and melodic motives.

Philip Glass hopes to create an aural freedom, a freedom from expecting something to happen, but he requires the listener to have a maximum of patience and time. Because of his mixture of rock elements, mysticism, confusing titles and stage actions, and hypnotic repetitious music lasting for long periods, Glass has also aroused a maximum of interest.

Suggested Listening: *Einstein on the Beach*
"Company" (Kronos String Quartet, Nonesuch recording)

Charles Ives (1874-1954) was probably the most brilliant and strangest of American composers. His music is sometimes still difficult to understand and to listen to, yet he quoted familiar music, American folk songs and hymns, in his pieces. But to understand Ives one has to know his background.

His father was a bandleader who liked to experiment with sounds, such as the musical "noises" made when two bands marched towards each other from opposite ends of a square. He encouraged Charles in such explorations. Charles played drums in the band at 12, and his father taught him piano and cornet. At 13 he played organ and would improvise, sometimes combining several keys as a joke. At 17 he composed his *Variations on America* for organ, which sounds occasionally like a caliope gone sour since it uses polytonal music (two or more keys at once).

In 1894 he attended Yale, taking a regular academic course and studying organ and compositon. In 1898 he joined an insurance company and also was organist at a New York Presbyterian church. In 1907 he formed an insurance company, Ives and Myrick, which made him quite wealthy. In 1919 he wrote the *Concord Sonata* for piano. Each of its four movements described a great New England thinker: Emerson, Hawthorne, the Alcotts, and Thoreau. In one place he suggests using a strip of wood on the keys to create a cluster. It is quite technically difficult. He wrote his Third Symphony in 1911 and it won the Pulitzer Prize in 1947.

Ives constantly experimented with new sounds, such as quarter-tone music (pitches closer together than the half-tones or half-steps on the piano). He often placed a hymn, folk song, or Stephen Foster song in the midst of a dissonant passage, and used deliberate "off-key" singing. He believed that composed music should imtiate music as we often hear it.

In 1918 Ives suffered a heart attack and had to semi-retire from both his business and from composing. Ives lived his dual life as long as he was able, stuffing his compositions away in drawers. He was a virtual recluse on his farm in West Redding, and had given up composing by 1928.

Ives only gradually got recognition for his talent in the years before he died (1954). It took almost a half century for public taste to catch up to the adventuresome spirit of Charles Ives.

Suggested Listening: *Variations on America* for organ
Concord Sonata
"General William Booth Enters Into Heaven" (Song arranged for chorus and brass band)

Scott Joplin was the greatest ragtime composer, but it was not until the 1974 movie "The Sting" made his rag "The Entertainer" a hit that he received well-deserved acclaim.

Joplin was born in Texarkana (the border town between Texas and Arkansas) in 1868. He learned to play the piano at home, later studying with a local German teacher. At 17 he made his way to St. Louis playing piano in various establishments for a living. He went to school at George Smith College, a black college in Sedalia, Missouri. He composed marches and songs of the trite sort popular at the time, and published "Original Rag" in 1899. Also, in the same year, he published his most famous piece, "Maple Leaf Rag", named after the Maple Leaf Club, a dance-hall. His publisher John Stark believed in the future of rags and kept Joplin busy and earning enough that he could settle in St. Louis and compose.

Joplin believed that his own syncopated pieces could compete with European classical music, and could become the important American music. He wrote a ragtime ballet, *The Ragtime Dance*, in 1902, and a now-lost ragtime opera, *A Guest of Honor*, in 1903. In 1907 he went to New York and promoted his ragtime opera, *Treemonisha*, completed in 1911. It concerns a black baby found under a tree by a woman names Monisha. The last ten years of his life were spent composing and trying to promote *Treemonisha*. It was given one performance, without scenery or costumes, but was a failure. Joplin never recovered from this defeat, and died in 1917.

It was in the small, well-crafted, popular rags that he achieved his lasting fame. Such works as "Solace", "Pineapple Rag", "Maple Leaf Rag", and "The Entertainer" have made his name known to several generations. In 1976 he was awarded a posthumous (after his death) Pulitzer Prize.

Suggested Listening: "Maple Leaf Rag"
"The Entertainer"
"Solace"

Francis Poulenc When one thinks of Francis Poulenc (pronounced Frahn-seese Poolank), the double masks of comedy and tragedy come to mind. In his compositions, he had the gift of tongue-in-cheek comedy and wit, as well as an instinct for supreme tragedy.

Poulenc (1899-1963) was born in Paris to wealthy parents. He began to study piano when he was five, and at 16 became a student of Ricardo Viñes, the Spanish concert pianist. The work which first made Poulenc known was *Rhapsodie Nègre* (1917), which had a vocal section of pseudo-African nonsense syllables. This tongue-in-cheek work and others attracted the attention of Erik Satie, the supremely witty and eccentric composer. He became associated with other followers of Satie, who rejected the phoney pompousness of most classical music. This young group, composed of Auric, Durey, Honegger, Milhaud, Tailleferre and Poulenc, became known as *Les Six* (pronounced Lay See). They attempted to simplify melody, harmony, and rhythm.

In the meantime Poulenc had served in the French Army (1918-21), studied composition with Charles Koechlin (1921-24), and was accompanist to the French baritone, Pierre Bernac. More Neo-Classical than his compatriots, Poulenc wrote a series of works which have made him perhaps the most important of the group. His works for piano include: *Trois mouvements perpétuels,* Sonata for two pianos, Sonata, for fourhands (1918), a fun student piece, *Concerto in D minor* for two pianos and orchestra, and *Concert Champetre* for harpsichord and orchestra. His vocal works include *Dialogues des Carmélites,* a tragic opera set in a nun's convent, now a staple in opera houses, and *La Voix humaine,* a monodrama for soprano solo.

Poulenc's most important contribution is in the field of song. He wrote more than 50 songs and song cycles (such as *Banalités*). His choral works are also important, including the *Stabat Mater*, and particularly the popular *Gloria,* for soprano, chorus and orchestra. His versatility may also be seen in his sparkling chamber works and in the humorous *Histoire de Babar le petit éléphant (History of Babar the Small Elephant) for narrator and piano.*

Poulenc's music has clarity and appeal. It is rich in lyrical melodies, dance-rhythms, and sumptuous scoring in a transparent French style. He was a versatile composer who charms amateurs and professionals alike, and is likely to grow in public esteem.

Suggested Listening: *Trois mouvements perpétuels*
Dialogues des Carmélites
Gloria

Sergei Prokofiev (1891-1953) was one of those rare child prodigies who continued to make a major contribution as an adult. He was born in a remote village in the Ukraine, Russia, where his father managed an estate. His mother encouraged his piano playing and improvising at an early age. In 1900, at the age of nine, he completed the piano score to an opera, The Giant. Many other compositions followed. He went to Moscow where he studied composition with Gliere. When the 13 year old arrived at the St. Petersburg Conservatory he had already written four operas, two sonatas, a symphony, and many piano pieces. There he studied composition with Rimsky-Korsakov. Prokofiev had a reputation as a rebel because of his percussive piano playing and satirical music. He graduated in 1914, winning the grand prize (The Anton Rubinstein prize was a grand piano).

He wrote the Classical Symphony in 1918, traveled to the U.S. and wrote the opera *Love for Three Oranges* for the Chicago Opera. From 1920-1932 he lived in Paris and collaborated with Diaghilev on ballet scores.

In 1933 he returned to Moscow to teach composition. When he arrived, the Communist Party had proclaimed the doctrine of socialist realism in the arts. Prokofiev thought he could continue writing forward-looking works, but his *Symphonic Song* was met with coldness while his music for the film *Lieutenant Kije* (1934) was successful. Learning to compromise, he turned to theater and film music, and *Alexander Nevsky* was the successful result.

His production was quite uneven. Sometimes he wrote bunches of boring political marches, other times he produced something as sublime as the ballet score *Romeo and Juliet.*

In spite of what Westerners saw as a stifling of his early imagination by the Soviet authorities, Prokofiev's biting harmonies, percussive rhythms, lyrical, soaring melodies and overall dramatic music continue to bring pleasure around the world.

Suggested Listening: *Classical Symphony*
Lieutenant Kije
Romeo and Juliet
Peter and the Wolf

Richard Rodgers was half of the famous Broadway musical composer team of Rodgers and Hammerstein. He was born in Hammels Station, Long Island, New York in 1902, and showed an early talent for music. He studied at Columbia University from 1919 to 1921, and there met his first collaborator, Lorenz "Larry" Hart. They jointly wrote the 1918 Varsity Show at Columbia, *Fly With Me,* but after that, success eluded them. Rodgers was about to give up music when *Garrick Gaieties* became a hit (1925). There followed a series of popular musical comedies: *The Girl Friend* (1926), *A Connecticut Yankee* (1927) (based on Mark Twain's story), *On Your Toes* (1936), containing the ballet "Slaughter on Tenth Avenue", *Babes in Arms* (1937), *I Married an Angel* (1938), *Pal Joey* (1940) (based on John O'Hara's New Yorker stories), and *The Boy From Syracuse* (1942).

When Larry Hart died in 1943, Rodgers found his great collaborator, Oscar Hammerstein II, who was already famous for his work with Sigmund Romberg and Jerome Kern. Rodgers and Hammerstein stormed Broadway with *Oklahoma!* (1943). It won a Pulitzer Prize in 1944 and played in New York for six years, holding a record for the longest run on Broadway for some time. Agnes de Mille, the great choreographer created the dances for *Oklahoma!* and for their next hit, *Carousel.* Other hit productions were *South Pacific* (1948, Pulitzer Prize winner in 1950), *The King and I* (1951), and *The Sound of Music* (1959). All of these musicals were made into hit movies, and songs from them, such as "Some Enchanted Evening" "Getting to Know You" and "Do Re Mi" became popular, too.

Rodgers also collaborated with Sondheim in *Do I Hear a Waltz,* and wrote the music for the television shows *Victory at Sea* (1952) and *Winston Churchill: The Valiant Years* (1960). He died a successful and honored man in New York in 1979.

Suggested Listening: *Oklahoma!*
Carousel
South Pacific
The King and I
The Sound of Music

Arnold Schoenberg (pronounced Schurn-bairg) (1874-1951) profoundly changed the course of music history by developing a substitute for the tonal system which composers had used for centuries.

He was largely self-taught. At an early age he learned to play cello and violin. When he was 16, his father died and he had to take a job as a bank clerk. He also earned extra money arranging songs and orchestrating operettas, something he had to do sporadically for some time to make ends meet.

In 1899 he wrote his first masterpiece, *Verklärte Nacht* (Transfigured Night), a story of two lovers. It was strongly influenced by Wagnerian harmonies. Around 1900 he was a conductor of several amateur choral gorups. He wrote the huge work *Gurrelieder* (Songs of Gurre) from 1901-1910. It called for three male choruses and an eight-part mixed chorus.

For a while, Schoenberg wrote songs for a cabaret in Berlin. He also taught at the Vienna Academy and at the Stern Conservatory in Berlin. In 1907 a riot broke out at the performance of his Chamber Symphony. In 1912 audience reaction was negative to Five Orchestra Pieces, and also for *Pierrot Lunaire,* a cycle of 21 songs for voice and chamber group accompaniment. In *Pierrot Lunaire* he used *sprechstimme,* a gliding speech-song, and no longer used a certain key (called atonal music).

Europe became increasingly difficult for Jews. Schoenberg came to the U. S., settled in Los Angeles, and taught at the University of Southern California, and at the University of California, Los Angeles. He developed his remarkable twelve-tone theory. An order of 12 pitches was arbitrarily selected, and this was used as the tool of composition rather than a scale. The Violin Concerto, Piano Concerto, and A Survivor from Warsaw all used the twelve-tone technique.

Schoenberg continued to struggle until the end of his life. He had little income, and audiences rejected his work, often booing and hissing. But history has accorded him his place of honor, as probably the most important composer of this century.

Suggested Listening: *Verklärte Nacht* (Transfigured Night)
       "Song of the Wood-Dove" from *Gurrelieder*
       Pierrot Lunaire
       A Survivor from Warsaw

Dimitri Shostakovich Shostakovich, the true Soviet composer, was born in St. Petersburg (Leningrad), Russia, in 1906 to a cultured, educated family. His father was a government engineer and his mother a professional pianist. His mother taught him piano before sending him to the Conservatory. While he was there, famine and disease hit the city and Shostakovich suffered malnutrition. The Conservatory authorities had to appeal for special aid to provide Shostakovich with the proper food. He graduated in 1925 having written the Symphony No. 1 in F minor as his diploma piece. He wrote a satirical opera, *The Nose,* which featured an interlude for percussion only.

His opera *Lady Macbeth of the District of Mtzensk* drew criticism from the Soviet authorities. It depicted "depravity", adultery, murder, and suicide under the Czars, but the adultery scenes shocked the officials, who chastised him. Shostakovich submitted an apology and pledged to write music according to acceptable standards, but his next theater work, *The Limpid Brook,* and his fourth Symphony were also condemned. It was only with his fifth Symphony in 1937 that Shostakovich was accepted. In 1948 Shostakovich was once again discredited by the Communist Party, the order rescinded only after Stalin's death in 1953. Once more in 1962 he was criticized by Krushchev for his Thirteenth Symphony. From then on, however, until his death in 1975, his music was gradually returned to the concert stage, and even works which had been condemned earlier were accepted and, received many honors. The Soviet Post Office issued a stamp in his honor on his 70th birthday. Shostakovich's music uses intricate counterpoint, strong rhythmic pulse, dissonant harmonies, and above all, dramatic power. His symphonies No. 1 and 5, particularly, have become popular in the U.S. His conductor son, Maxim, defected to the U.S. in 1981 and continues to bring his father's music to the western world.

Suggested Listening: Symphony No. 1
       Symphony No. 5
       Lady Macbeth of the District Mtzensk

Stephen Joshua Sondheim was born in New York in 1930. He attended George School, a private school in Newtown, Pennsylvania, where he met James Hammerstein, the son of

Oscar Hammerstein II. James took his 15 year old friend and would-be musical comedy composer to meet his father. Sondheim brought some music at which Hamemrstein was kind enough to look . Hammerstein served for several years as critic and mentor. Sondheim entered Williams College as a music major and decided to make his career in the theater. After graduating magna cum laude (with honors) in 1950, he was awarded a prize to study with Milton Babbitt, the famous composer. He supported himself by writing the scripts for the television series, *Topper*.

Through the playwright Arthur Laurents, Sondheim was introduced to Leonard Bernstein, who needed a lyricist for *West Side Story*. Sondheim got the job, and the 27 year old's reputation was made with that work. Sondheim next collaborated with Jule Styne on *Gypsy,* still providing the lyrics.

With *A Funny Thing Happened on the Way to the Forum,* starring Zero Mostel, Sondheim finally had a chance to write both the music and lyrics. In 1964 his show *Anyone Can Whistle* flopped, but in that show he began to use a trademark—accompaniments which betray the true feelings of the character even though the words say something else.

Sondheim wrote lyrics for *Do I Hear A Waltz?,* with music by Richard Rodgers, and then wrote both music and lyrics for *Company, Follies,* and *A Little Night Music* (based on the Ingmar Bergman film), all successes. Another failure occurred in 1976— *Pacific Overtures*—despite its sumptious scenery and costumes. The musical revue *Side by Side* by Sondheim, was produced, and showcased all of Sondheim's hits to date.

With *Sweeney Todd,* 1979, Sondheim entered new territory. The score earned high praise for its almost operatic scale, but the story of a vicious murderer was repulsive to many. The audience was slightly uncomfortable at the truth of the human condition, as they often are in a Sondheim production.

In 1984 he completed *Sunday in the Park with George,* based on George Seurat's painting, again to mixed reviews. The musical was awarded the Pulitzer Prize for drama.

Stephen Sondheim, at 57, has managed to write complex, dramatic, and thought-provoking musicals, and shows promise of more to come.

Suggested Listening: *A Funny Thing Happened on the Way to the Forum*
A Little Night Music (especially "Send in the Clowns")
Company

Igor Stravinsky was one of the two most important masters of twentieth-century music. He and Arnold Schoenberg are considered the two who have shaped the course of history. (Interestingly, both men lived their last years close by in Los Angeles, California, but never associated with each other.)

Stravinsky was born near St. Petersburg, Russia in 1882, the son of a distinguished bass opera singer. As a young boy he loved the theater and attended rehearsals with his father. He studied piano and theory, but was very slow in composition. In 1901 he enrolled at the law school in St. Petersburg, but did not graduate. There he met the son of Rimsky-Korsakov and in 1905 he began orchestration lessons with Rimsky-Korsakov.

An important event in Stravinsky's life occurred when the famous impressario Diaghilev asked Stravinsky to write a work for his Ballet Russes, performing in Paris. Stravinsky used a Russian fairy tale, pulsating rhythms, and rich harmonies and orchestration. The result in 1910 was *The Firebird*. Stravinsky now found himself collaborating with Diaghilev and moved to Paris in 1911. His second ballet, *Petrouchka,* about a tragic puppet, used two keys simultaneously (C and F-sharp) and was a great success. In 1913 he produced such a stark and discordant work in Rite of Spring *(Le Sacre du Printemps)* that the audience rioted at such barbaric music.

When World War I curtailed lavish expenditures for large orchestras, Stravinsky wrote a series of chamber works: *L'Histoire du Soldat,* for narrator and seven musicians, *Ragtime,* and *Pulcinella.*

Next he entered a Neo-Classical phase, copying earlier styles and forms. *Apollon Musagete* was in the manner of a Lully court ballet, *Capriccio* for piano and orchestra, was in eighteenth-century style, and *Oedipus Rex,* a Greek play.

In 1939 Stravinsky moved to the U.S. In 1946 he wrote *Ebony Concerto* for a swing band. In 1951 he wrote one of his most important works, *The Rake's Progress,* in eighteenth-century style.

His last style period contained works written in the so-called twelve-tone technique, invented by Schoenberg. In this style no key is used, but an order, or row of pitches, arbitrarily picked, is used. Works in this period were *Agnon,* a Greek ballet, and *The Flood.*

Stravinsky lived a long (he died in 1971) and varied life in composition. He influenced others by his free surging rhythms, colorful harmonies, and brilliant orchestration.

Suggested Listening: *The Firebird*
Rite of Spring (Le Sacre du Printemps)
L'Histoire du Soldat

Ralph Vaughan Williams A key figure in English Nationalism, Ralph (the English say "Raif") Vaughan Williams created a new British style of composition which mixed native folk songs with modern harmony and orchestral color.

He was born in Down Ampney, Gloucestershire, England, in 1872. His father, a clergyman, died when he was a child. He moved with his family to his grandparents and began to study piano and violin there. When he was 15 he played violin and viola in his school orchestra. Education was important to his family and Vaughan Williams received a fine academic background. He attended the Royal College of Music where he studied composition with Parry and then went to Cambridge and graduated with two Bachelor's degrees in 1894 and 1895. In 1897 he went to Berlin, Germany to study with Max Bruch (famous for his violin concerto), and in 1901 he received his Doctor of Music at Cambridge. All of this was to prepare him for a career as an organist and church musician. But he was dissatisfied with his education. He began collecting English folk music, and then traveled to Paris to study orchestration with Ravel.

In 1919 he became a professor of composition at the Royal College of Music and devoted his time to composition, folk song research, and editing church music.

Noteworthy among his compositons are: *Toward the Unknown Region* (1906), a choral work inspired by the American poet Walt Whitman, *Fantasia on a Theme by Thomas Tallis* (1909), perhaps his most popular work, *A Sea Symphony* (1909), *A London Symphony* (1913), *The Lark Ascending* (revised 1920), for violin and orchestra, *A Pastoral Symphony* (1921), *Sinfonia Antartica* (1952), based on a movie score about Sir Robert Scott's South Pole Expedition, uses a wind machine.

Vaughan Williams lived a long and productive life (he died in 1958 at 86) promoting the use of folk music, developing church music, establishing a new choral tradition and using his prowess at orchestral color to create interesting and picturesque symphonic works.

Suggested Listening: *Toward the Unknown Region*
Fantasia on a Theme by Thomas Tallis
A Pastoral Symphony

APPENDIX

Careers In Music

A career in music can mean anything from teaching piano students to being an international rock star. It can be a full time pursuit, or a part-time addition to an individual's primary source of income. The music world is extremely diverse, and the possibilities are extremely varied. Like any other field, any person's chances of success are based on talent, organization, hard work and perception of the right opportunities on which to capitalize. Anyone in any life-long music career didn't just get there by chance. Even if a rare "discovery" occurs, the person has to be ready to be discovered. The time-worn advice to anyone who aspires to a life in any of the arts is: Prepare for your chance, and whenever it comes, be ready to accept it.

Although we first tend to think of only performing as a music career option, there actually are many other possibilities for interesting and exciting pursuits. The following is a list of some of these possibilities. If you are seriously intrigued by any of these ideas, contact a person who is in a similar role. Find out from them what their life is really like, what kind of preparation they recommend. You may find that you aren't interested after all. On the other hand, it could be a beginning to the achievement of a personal goal and a vocation for life.

You only have to take the first step.

Have you thought about these careers?

Private Teaching
   Full-time studio
   Conservatory teacher
   Store/Studio teacher
   Class instructor
Teaching in Schools
   Elementary Choral teacher
   Junior High Choral teacher
   Senior High Choral teacher
   General Music teacher
   Elementary Instrumental teacher
   Junior High Instrumental teacher
   Senior High Instrumental teacher
University or College Teaching
   Applied Music (private instruction)
   Musicology
   Music Theory and related subjects
   Pedagogy
   Music Education teacher
   Ensemble conductor
   Administrator
   Artist/teacher
Performing in Commercial Music
   Recording studio performer
   Free-lance artist
   Solo recording

Back-up singer
Film and TV studio work
Theatre
Composer/Arranger
   Free-lance publishing
   Commissioned work
   Commercial Arranging
   Music for Theatre
   Film/TV scoring
   Free-lance arranging
Music Related Careers
   Music critic
   Broadcasting
   Artist management
   Arts management
   Music Librarian
   Theatre technician
   Arts writer
   Instrument repair
Church music
   Choir Director
   Organist
   Soloist and/or section leader
Conducting
   Civic and Youth Orchestras
   Choral Conductor

Opera Conductor
Musical Theatre
Ballet Conductor
Symphony Conductor
Commercial Conductor for film or TV
Performing Art Music
Free-lance performer
Orchestral player
Professional Choral Ensemble singer
Opera singer
Solo Concert Artist
Accompanying/coaching
Recording Industry
Recording Technician
Producer
Administrator

Disc jockey
Public Relations
Advertising/promotion
Video Production
Music Publishing
Arranger
Editor
Copyright worker
Sales/Promotion
Management
Accounting
Graphics
Music in Business
Entertainment Industry Law
Music Retail
Instrument manufacturing